Jennifer Aldridge's

Archers'
COUNTRY
KITCHEN

should be
made in
double boiler
Lemon
If you want a dressing
this is what we used

Jennifer Aldridge's

Archers'
COUNTRY
KITCHEN

D&C
David and Charles

For the smallest and newest –
Lily and Montie with my love.

A DAVID & CHARLES BOOK
Copyright © David & Charles Limited 2011

David & Charles is an imprint of F&W Media International, LTD
Brunel House, Forde Close, Newton Abbot, TQ12 4PU, UK

F&W Media International, LTD is a subsidiary of F+W Media Inc. , 10151 Carver Road, Suite #200,
Blue Ash, OH 45242, USA

First published in the UK in 2011

Text copyright © Angela Piper 2011
Photographs copyright © see p. 176
Illustrations copyright © Mary Woodin 2011

ISBN-13: 978-1-4463-0251-4 hardback
ISBN-10: 1-4463-0251-2 hardback

Printed in China by RR Donnelley
for F&W Media International, LTD
Brunel House, Forde Close, Newton Abbot, TQ12 4PU, UK

Publishing Director: Ali Myer
Art Editor: Prudence Rogers
Design Direction: Angela Piper
Project Editor: Emily Pitcher
Editor: Sarah Callard
Production Controller: Bev Richardson

F±W Media publishes high quality books on a wide range of subjects.
For more great book ideas visit: www.rubooks.co.uk

Contents

Introduction

'*That's saved my life Jenny darling*' *sighed Lilian, licking a fleck of foam from a skinny-latte off her glossy pink lips, while flicking away a stray muffin crumb perched on her cream cashmere cardigan. We gathered together our wits and stiff smart carrier bags, struggled onto our designer heels and teetered through the chatteringly crowded coffee shop. Ahead of us in the neon-clinical brilliance of Underwoods' expensive and expansive kitchen department stood a startling array of sturdy, shining stacks of saucepans and stewpans, milkpans and measuring jugs. Regimented rows of graters and grinders, bowls and balloon whisks and gleaming glass goblets. A veritable world of whirling and whirring culinary wizardry and stainless steel sterility. All up-to-the-minute 'must-haves' in this 21st century of cunning invention and super-sharpened speedy electrical efficiency. But somehow this yawningly vast near-vapid void seems devoid of life's most crucial yearnings. Where are those teasing, tempting nose-ticklingly enticing sweet and spicy scents that would mysteriously and magically quench my memory's thirst? There before us, lo and behold, a pyramid of little pots, a tower of teetering tins, all with wax and wicks awaiting their flickering into perfumed flames, all seducing us into a virtual life.*

Here's one...

SWEET ORANGE AND CITRUS BURST –
with a hint of Mediterranean magic

Let me just remember that cold grey January day at Brookfield, as the wind whipped round the yard and raindrops spattered on the window panes. Gran and I

basked in the cosiness of her kitchen, the preserving pan bubbling and spluttering on the hob, the sweet citrussy steam filling the air. I was allowed to lick the sticky wooden spoon as Gran ladled the tawny, chunky preserve into squeaky clean jars. Soon after, those frilly-topped pots were labelled, ranged and displayed on her cool larder shelves. 'There, that's sunshine in a jar,' she smiled.

PINK PETAL BOUQUET – *the fragrance of your flower garden*

Not just sweet memories of Mum's charming garden at Blossom Hill Cottage, but the day I helped pick perfumed old-fashioned roses for her pink petal sorbet. It had been one of those perfect June days with a pastel blue sky shimmering with promise, bees droning and dozily nuzzling the fragrant blooms. Inside her low-beamed kitchen the scented steam relaxed and soothed us both. 'If only your dad could see us both now,' she sighed.

SUGARY CINNAMON STICK –
full of exotic, Eastern, promise

I remember it was more practical than exotic the promise made by the Grundy boys at Grange Farm one windy, wintery evening. A floury and flustered Clarrie answered the door to my 'coo-ee' with a welcoming smile and a warm waft of cinnamon and spice. Young Edward and William were sent packing to gather kindling for the stove. 'You promised, you two – or there'll be no cake for your tea'.
  'Close the door will you, Clarrie?' growled grumpy old Joe from his jealously-guarded corner of the kitchen by the stove. 'When the wind is in the east, 'tis neither good for man nor beast,' he muttered.

PUMPKINS

pumpkin seeds to roast.

...ace them on a tray with olive oil sea salt

PLUM PIE – *memories of an orchard's fragrance*

I don't just remember the plump fruit picked from laden, bee-buzzing branches, but more the memory of gentle Auntie Pru in her quintessential country kitchen. There was always a colourful jumble of jars of homemade jam, tall slim bottles of clear cordials and pot upon chubby chunky pot of chutneys, pickles and sharp, sweet jellies. Bristling bunches of herbs twizzled from low oak beams, and Pru wouldn't have been Pru without her delicious puddings and prize-winning cakes. Plump, portly Uncle Tom was proof of her prowess. 'I am proud of myself, really proud' she whispered when she won a 1st for the lightest, most feathery sponge at Ambridge's Flower & Produce Show many years ago.

MELLOW FRUITS – *with just a hint of autumn*

There was definitely more than just a hint of autumn when I stepped inside the door at Brookfield Bungalow. 'Whoops, mind where you tread' warned cheery, overalled Freda bumping into a hessian bag bulging with Bert's late-croppers. We stepped over wicker-woven baskets wedged with earthy vegetables. I spotted crinkly, grey-green cabbages and sternly striped marrows awaiting dissection on the drainer by the sink. I breathed in the mellowness of apples picked on those gloriously golden September days, saw ringlets of peel spilled on the table's oil cloth top and smelled the spicy sweetness seeping from a buttery bubbling pan of Bert's prized pumpkin. Freda flapped her tea towel at some dozy wasps buzzing round the stove. 'The drowsy wasps hum loud and long. A slow and mournful autumn song.'
  'My Bert's never lost for a rhyme', she chuckled.

STRAWBERRY SUNDAE – *the sweetness of summer*

Oh yes, there is the promise of delicious sweetness this summer, and here are the baskets and bowls spilling at the brim with their luscious, scarlet berries. This the glorious glut of summer's succulent strawberries. After pink-stained fingers have patiently picked and carefully plucked each individual rosy fruit, there's hulling, occasional careless squashing, and the inevitable sampling of Adam's successful Home Farm harvest. The homecoming from Africa of Adam, my first-born very special son, has filled me with great happiness. I've loved these lengthy summer days offering hours of sunshine, picnics, jolly jaunts, fresh air and freedom for all my children.

But right now I'm busy. I shall pick over, purée and pot, strain and sweeten for syrups; I'll bake puddings and pies, boil jellies and jams, make preparations for the inevitability of autumn in both my now happy home and our comfortable lives. As the great bard said, 'summer's lease hath all too short a date' I mused...

A tap on my shoulder jerked me back to reality. 'Oh come on Jenny, let's get going. Do hurry up, my feet are killing me.' I put down the teasingly-scented wax-filled tin and headed purposefully to the swinging doors of Underwoods' tempting store, but hardly hearing Lilian shrilly calling 'Just something for supper…it's last on my list…you know, quick and easy… boil-in-the-bag…pre-cooked, pre-packed, foil-wrapped…' Oh no, Lilian! No!

Instead I headed back and escaped down Borsetshire's winding lanes. There, in the comfort of my farmhouse home, I riffled in drawers and poked into boxes, finding cards and old calendars, cuttings and snippings, notelets and jottings – even funny old photos that I knew I'd forgotten. Just a glorious jumble of colourful memories. This is my personal pot pourri of our country kitchens.

Jennifer.

AUTUMN

Autumn is upon us – heavy-beaded dew, misty mornings and golden afternoons bestow the countryside's seasonal bounty. Along the Little Croxley Lane, bee-droning hedgerows are bedecked with gleaming, tawny berries. Plums hang plump and ripe in ladder-leaning orchards, while wicker baskets brim with crisp, green apples. This glorious glut is transformed in bubbling pans to claret-coloured jellies, chunky chutneys and syrupy jam. A veritable kaleidoscope of colourful globes arranged in regimented rows on Ambridge pantry shelves.

High Tea at Brookfield

Ham & egg pie ✓

Cold roast beef ✓

Pickled beetroot and horseradish sauce ✓

Homebaked bread ✓

Treacle tart ✓

Date and walnut loaf ✓

Tea ✓

september 195

1ᴰ HOME COOKERY 1ᴰ

Chintz curtains close out the fast-fading light and the hall clock strikes six. In from the chilly yard, Dan and Phil, greeted by the cosy warmth of the farmhouse kitchen, chat cheerfully about the cost of autumn calvers. Doris cuts crusty wedges of her cottage loaf while Christine slices succulent cold roast beef onto willow-pattern plates. In pride of place on the gingham cloth sits a plump pork pie accompanied by jars of Gran's pickled beetroot and creamy horseradish sauce. A crumbly, syrupy treacle tart, bubblingly hot from the oven, and buttered date and walnut loaf follow with steaming cups of tea. This is a typical tea at Brookfield Farm.

SEPTEMBER

BEST PILCHARD BAKE

8 tinned pilchards
salt and pepper
1 onion
4 bay leaves
½ pint ale
1 tsp of cloves
1 tsp ground allspice
a basin-full of cold mashed potato

Sprinkle salt and pepper on the fish, and put in an ovenware dish. Slice the onion thinly and scatter the rings on the fish, together with the bay leaves. Pour over the ale and add the cloves and allspice. Cover with the mashed potato and bake at 350ºF for 1 hour. Serve hot or cold.

1 SAT PARTRIDGE SHOOTING BEGINS	**2** SUN
5 WED	**6** THU
9 SUN	**10** MON

13 THU	**14** FRI	**15** SAT	**16** SUN	**17** MON
19 WED	**20** THU	**21** FRI	**22** SAT	**23** SUN
25 TUE	**26** WED	**27** THU	**28** FRI	**29** SAT MICHAELMAS

3 MON	**4** TUE

7 FRI	**8** SAT

1 TUE	**12** WED

SPICED PICKLED PEARS

3½lb Comice or Conference pears, peeled, cored and quartered
½ stick of cinnamon
1 tsp grated nutmeg
4 cloves
1½lb sugar
½ pint vinegar

Put the spices in a muslin bag and place with all the ingredients in a heavy-bottomed saucepan. Add enough water to cover the pears. Bring to the boil and simmer gently for about 20 minutes until the pears are soft (keep in quarters). Place the pears in clean jars. Boil the cooking syrup for 20 minutes longer to reduce and thicken. Pour the syrup over the pears, then place and tie down the lids when cold. Delicious with cold lamb.

8 UE

24 MON

30 SUN

PLOUGHMAN'S PUDDING

4oz stale bread
½ pint milk, boiling
4oz beef suet
4oz mixed dried fruit
1 tsp mixed spice
pinch of salt
3 eggs
2oz sugar

Soak the bread in milk until it is absorbed. Stir in the suet, dried fruit, mixed spice and salt. Whisk the eggs with the sugar and add to the other ingredients. Pour into a greased pudding basin. Cover with greaseproof paper, and then a pudding cloth. Tie down firmly and boil for 2 hours.

Shane's Kitchen Garden Striped Terrine

Shane, silent as always, served Nelson's customers with distinctive style, slicing and scooping, stirring and spooning his sweet desserts and savoury creations.

SERVES 10 AS A FIRST COURSE,
6 AS A MAIN COURSE

550g (1½lb) **parsnips, peeled, cored
and cut into chunks**
550g (1½lb) **carrots, peeled and chopped**
550g (1½lb) **spinach leaves**
3 **eggs**
90ml (3fl oz) **crème fraîche**
½ tsp **ground mace**
½ tsp **ground coriander**
salt and pepper

Preheat the oven to 160°C/325°F/Gas 3. Butter a 900g (2lb) loaf tin and line the base with greaseproof paper. Cook the parsnips and carrots in separate saucepans of water until tender, then drain thoroughly. Wash the spinach, removing the stalks, and place in a saucepan with only the water clinging to its leaves. Cook over a low heat for 5 minutes until it wilts and softens, then drain well. Purée each of the vegetables and then return them to their individual pans and heat gently, stirring, until the excess liquid has evaporated. Cool slightly, then add an egg and 2 tablespoons of crème fraîche to each purée and mix well. Season each with salt and pepper, adding the mace to the carrots and the coriander to the parsnips.

Spoon the parsnip purée into the loaf tin, levelling it to make a smooth layer, followed by the carrot and finally the spinach purée. Cover with a piece of foil, place the tin in a roasting tin half filled with hot water and bake for about 1½ hours or until a skewer inserted in the centre comes out clean. Remove from the oven and leave to cool before turning out carefully on to a serving plate. This terrine can be served with a tomato or red pepper sauce, or with Jean-Paul's Green Tomato Jam.

Bert's Best Tips:
At the end of September there's an Indian summer when North American Indians stored their crops for the winter

Jean-Paul's Green Tomato Jam

(Confiture de Tomates Vertes)

This is transformed into a delicious dessert when served with crème fraîche. Jean-Paul, the erstwhile chef at Grey Gables, imbued with a fair share of French arrogance, insisted it should be eaten with soft goat's cheese, a dash of rum and a sprinkling of sugar – 'naturellement!'

MAKES 2–2.5KG (4–5LB)

1.5kg (3lb) green tomatoes
1kg (2½lb) granulated sugar or preserving sugar
2 limes, sliced

Wash the tomatoes and slice them very thinly crosswise. Layer them in a bowl with the sugar and sliced limes, then cover and leave for 24 hours. Transfer the mixture to a preserving pan and heat slowly until boiling. Simmer gently, stirring frequently, for about 1 hour. When the mixture turns a golden colour, test for setting point: put a teaspoonful on a saucer, place in the fridge for a minute or two and then gently push the jam with your finger – if it wrinkles, it has reached setting point. Skim, leave for 5 minutes, then pour into sterilised jars and seal while hot.

Autumn Chestnut and Orange Soup

After gathering bulging pocketfuls of sweet chestnuts while autumn walking in the Country Park, what could be nicer than making this warming soup? Actually, roasting the chestnuts in the ashes of the log fire and scooping them up, blackened and popping, is much more fun!

SERVES 8

450g (1lb) whole chestnuts
35g (1½oz) butter
1 onion, peeled and chopped
2 carrots, peeled and chopped
1 tsp flour
finely grated zest and juice of 1 large orange
1 litres (1¾ pints) chicken stock
  (or bouillon)
salt and pepper

Either roast the chestnuts or soak in boiling water for 5 minutes. Remove the shell and inner skins. Melt the butter in a large saucepan and sauté the onion and carrots until soft and golden. Add the flour and stir until it begins to colour. Stir in the chestnuts, orange zest, juice and stock. Season, then cover and simmer for 35 minutes, or until the chestnuts are tender. Purée the soup in a blender, and re-heat to serve.

Kept warm in a flask, this is just the soup for a winter picnic. 'Just an extra slug of sherry in it, darling, is what it needs' was Lilian's passing comment!

Hunky Chunky Bread

After rolling up sleeves and washing hands, Phoebe and Ruairi loved the silky feeling of the flour as they rubbed in the cold chunks of butter.

MAKES 1 LOAF

450g (1lb) plain flour
1 tsp salt
1 tsp bicarbonate of soda
25g (1oz) butter
about 300ml (½ pint) skimmed milk

Heat the oven to 220°C/425°F/Gas 7. Sift the flour, salt and bicarbonate of soda into a big bowl and rub in the butter with your fingers, until it resembles breadcrumbs. Make a hollow in the centre and stir in the milk. Keep stirring until you have a soft mixture that isn't sticking to the inside of the bowl. Sprinkle some flour onto a clean surface and tip this mixture onto it. Pat it into a round shape about 2.5cm (1in) thick. Carefully put the dough onto a greased baking tin and, with a knife, make a deep cross on top of the loaf. Bake for about 35 minutes until golden and it sounds hollow when tapped on the underside.

This bread can be eaten hot straight from the oven with butter and honey, or a lump of cheese. Or, for a warming lunchtime treat, try it with my pumpkin soup.

Pumpkin Soup

Ruairi was delighted to discover a golden globe of a pumpkin left on our doormat by Bert one misty October morning. Brian helped him to carve a lantern while I whizzed up this delicious soup.

SERVES 6

1 pumpkin
2 potatoes
55g (2oz) butter
600ml (1 pint) milk
300ml (½ pint) water
salt and pepper
a little grated nutmeg

Slice the top off the pumpkin. Scrape out the flesh with a sharp spoon and cut it into small pieces. Peel the potatoes and cut these also into small pieces. Melt the butter in a large pan, add the pumpkin and potato and stir. Add the milk and water and cook on a slow heat for about 25 minutes. Season to taste, add the nutmeg and mix into a smooth soup with an electric blender or rub through a sieve. Serve with hunky chunky bread.

Freda Fry's Pumpkin Pie with Walnut Crust

The rest of Bert's pampered pumpkin crop is put to good use by his clever wife. 'Just in time for harvest supper,' said Freda, flushed and floury-fingered at the end of the day's baking.

SERVES 4–6

900g (2lb) pumpkin, before trimming
55g (2oz) unsalted butter
115g (4oz) soft brown sugar
pinch of salt
1 tsp ground cinnamon
½ tsp ground ginger
½ tsp grated nutmeg
2 eggs, beaten
150ml (5fl oz) double cream

For the pastry:
115g (4oz) plain flour
1 tbsp icing sugar
pinch of salt
75g (3oz) chilled butter
55g (2oz) walnuts, finely chopped
1 egg
2 tbsp cold water

To make the pastry, sift the flour, icing sugar and salt into a large mixing bowl, then grate in the butter and stir in the walnuts. Whisk the egg with the cold water and add to the pastry mixture. Stir with a fork until the mixture holds together, adding a little more water if necessary. Knead lightly, then wrap in cling film and chill for 30 minutes. Preheat the oven to 180°C/350°F/Gas 4.

Meanwhile, make the filling: remove the seeds and skins from the pumpkin and chop the flesh into chunks. Melt the butter in a large saucepan over a low heat. Add the flesh, cover and cook until soft, stirring occasionally. After 15 minutes or so, remove the lid to allow most of the liquid to evaporate. Purée the pumpkin in a food processor with the sugar, salt, spices, eggs and cream.

Roll out the pastry and use to line a 20cm (8in) flan dish. Pour the pumpkin mixture into the pastry case and bake for 40–45 minutes, until the filling is set.

Gibson's Amazing Chickpea Bake

Gibson, that gloriously good-looking college chum of Kate's, lived for a very short time in one of Home Farm's holiday cottages. They entertained us one evening and Brian and I just can't remember a meal we have enjoyed more.

SERVES 4

225g (8oz) chickpeas
2 tbsp olive oil
2 onions, peeled and chopped
5 garlic cloves, peeled and halved
115g (4oz) mushrooms, chopped
225g (8oz) small turnips, peeled and chopped
225g (8oz) carrots, peeled and sliced
4 cloves
½ cinnamon stick
large sprig of thyme
150ml (5fl oz) vegetable stock
150ml (5fl oz) red wine
salt and pepper

Soak the chickpeas in water to cover overnight, then drain. Cover with fresh water, bring to the boil and simmer until tender, then drain again (alternatively, used tinned chickpeas that are already cooked).

Preheat the oven to 180°C/350°F/Gas 4. Heat the oil in a large, heavy-based saucepan over a low heat. Add the onions and garlic and cook, stirring, until they begin to brown but not burn. Stir in all the vegetables and cook for a few minutes, then transfer to a casserole dish. Stir in the chickpeas, spices, thyme, stock and wine and season well with salt and pepper. Cover and bake for 1½ hours. Serve on a bed of healthy brown rice.

Thyme – Thym

Strong aromatic herb – many varieties

Use in forcemeats, stuffings and soups

Helen's Healthy Lentil Bake

Vegetables straight from Ambridge Organics are used in this wholesome recipe.

SERVES 4

2 carrots, peeled and finely diced
2 parsnips, peeled and finely diced
225g (8oz) spilt red lentils
25g (1oz) butter
1 onion, finely chopped
25g (1oz) plain flour
300ml (½ pint) milk
1 tsp Dijon mustard
55g (2oz) Cheshire or Borsetshire
  cheese, grated
2 tbsp wholemeal breadcrumbs
25g (1oz) mixed nuts, chopped
salt and pepper

Cook the carrots and parsnips in boiling salted water until tender, and then drain. Cook the lentils in boiling water for 15–20 minutes, until tender, then drain and mix with the carrots and parsnips.

Melt the butter in a saucepan and sauté the onion for 2–3 minutes, until softened. Stir in the flour, cook for 1–2 minutes and then gradually stir in the milk. Cook, stirring, until the sauce thickens and bubbles. Stir in the mustard and the lentil mixture and season to taste. Simmer until heated through. Pour into individual flameproof dishes, sprinkle with the cheese, breadcrumbs and nuts and brown under a hot grill.

Get rid of mice by stopping up the holes with a large cork dipped in water and cayenne pepper

Home Farm Game Pie

If my freezer hadn't been full of Tom's excellent pork I would have used venison in this pie – cut in smaller chunks and marinated in red wine overnight.

SERVES 8

450g (1lb) pork, cut into 2.5cm (1in) cubes
450g (1lb) boned pheasant, cut into 2.5cm (1in) cubes
1 tbsp plain flour
2 tsp chopped thyme
2 tbsp orange marmalade
grated zest of 1 lemon
4 tbsp Madeira
450g (1lb) ham, cut into 2.5cm (1in) cubes
4 tbsp chopped parsley
1 tsp grated nutmeg
1 egg yolk, beaten with 1 tbsp water, to glaze
salt and pepper

For the pastry:
450g (1lb) plain flour
1 tsp salt
225g (8oz) lard
150ml (5fl oz) water

To make the pastry, sift the flour and salt into a bowl and make a well in the centre. Put the lard into a saucepan with the water, heat until just boiling, then tip into the flour, stirring with a wooden spoon. Beat to form a smooth dough, then turn onto a floured surface and knead gently for a minute. Cover and leave for 30 minutes.

Meanwhile, prepare the filling: mix together the pork, pheasant, flour, thyme, marmalade, lemon zest and Madeira. Season with salt and pepper. In a separate bowl, mix together the ham, parsley and nutmeg and season to taste.

Preheat the oven to 220°C/425°F/Gas 7. Roll out three-quarters of the pastry and use to line a 900g (2lb) loaf tin. Spoon half the pork and pheasant mixture into the tin and press down lightly. Cover with the ham mixture and arrange the remaining pork and pheasant on top, pressing down to fill the tin. Dampen the pastry edges with a little water. Roll out the remaining pastry to form a lid, put it on top of the pie and press the edges together to seal. Make small vents along the top of the pie, then bake in the centre of the oven for 15 minutes. Brush the top of the pie with the egg yolk glaze, then lower the temperature to 180°C/350°F/Gas 4 and continue cooking for 1½ hours. Leave to cool completely. Then chill (overnight if possible) before turning out on to a serving plate.

Bar au Loup de Mer au Fenouil

Sea bass, with its delicious, moist flesh, was roasted over a bed of fennel for Alice and Christopher's special post-wedding celebration barbecue. I managed to twist the chef's arm for his superb recipe, which works just as well in a traditional oven as it does on the barbecue.

SERVES 6

3 tbsp roughly chopped parsley
2 garlic cloves, peeled and chopped
finely grated zest and juice of 1 large lemon
2 tsp chopped or grated root ginger
2 sea bass (around 300g/½lb) each
1 handful fennel fronds
4 tbsp olive oil
salt

Preheat the grill to medium. Mix together the parsley, garlic, lemon zest and ginger, and stuff this into the cavity of the fish. Make 3 or 4 cuts in the side of the fish and tuck the fennel into the cuts. Brush the fish with olive oil and lemon juice, and sprinkle with salt. Cook under the grill for 12–15 minutes, basting from time to time.

This is served with the piquante Sauce Verte.

Sauce Verte

handful each of spinach, watercress,
  parsley, chervil and tarragon
2 tbsp (30ml) mayonnaise
salt and pepper
juice of 1 lemon

Blanche the spinach, watercress and herbs in boiling water for 1 minute. Remove from the pan, and transfer to iced water to cool. Pat dry.

Place the mayonnaise in a food processor and add the herbs. Process until the sauce is smooth and the herbs finely chopped. Test the seasoning, and add a little lemon juice if necessary.

Pommes de Terre Persillées – Parsley Potatoes

SERVES 6

450g (1lb) potatoes, peeled
55g (2oz) butter
2 large garlic cloves, thinly sliced
1 bunch spring onions, thinly sliced
3 tbsp chopped parsley
salt and pepper
150ml (5fl oz) double cream
75ml (2½fl oz) crème fraîche

Preheat the oven to 190°C/375°F/Gas 5. Slice the potatoes thinly. Butter an ovenproof dish and place a layer of potatoes on the bottom. Sprinkle with some garlic, spring onions and parsley, then season well. Continue to make more layers of potatoes, parsley and seasoning, finishing with a layer of potatoes. Dot with the remaining butter, mix the crème fraîche and cream together and pour over. Bake for 50–60 minutes, until the potatoes are tender when a knife is inserted.

Tarragon – Estragon

Protect from frost –
a summer herb

Mild seasoning with an aniseed flavour

Use in lightly-cooked vegetables,
or herb vinegar for salads

Clarrie's Scrumpy and Cinnamon Cake

Everyone in Ambridge must surely know of Joe Grundy's potent home brew – his Grange Farm cider which he makes from wizened old windfalls. Clarrie tipped some into her cinnamon cake one day with superb results!

MAKES AN 18CM (7IN) CAKE

115g (4oz) butter or margarine
115g (4oz) soft light brown sugar
2 eggs, beaten
115g (4oz) self-raising flour

115g (4oz) wholemeal flour
1 tsp bicarbonate of soda
1 tsp ground cinnamon
175ml (6fl oz) cider

Preheat the oven to 180°C/350°F/Gas 4. Grease and line the base of an 18cm (7in) round cake tin. Beat the butter or margarine and sugar together until light and creamy, then gradually beat in the eggs. Fold in half of each flour with the bicarbonate of soda and cinnamon, then fold in the cider and the remaining flour. Turn into the prepared tin and bake for 35–40 minutes, until the cake is springy to the touch and shrinking away from the sides of the tin. Cool in the tin for 10 minutes, then turn out on to a wire rack to cool completely.

Auntie Pru's Plum and Walnut Crisp with Cinnamon Cream

Such a simple pudding, I suggested it to Alice when she discovered some slightly stale brioche lurking in the bottom of the bread crock. Maybe she can try to impress the Carters with it one day.

SERVES 6

85g (3oz) butter
175g (6oz) brioche, crumbed
85g (3oz) soft brown sugar
55g (2oz) chopped walnuts
450g (1lb) plums

Preheat the oven to 180°C/350°F/Gas 4. Melt the butter and sugar together in a heavy-bottomed saucepan, and add in the brioche crumbs. Stir well to coat the crumbs, and then add the walnuts and gently cook for a couple of minutes, stirring occasionally so that it doesn't catch. Remove from the heat. Cut the plums in half, removing the stones, and poach lightly in water. When soft, put the plums into a pie dish and allow to cool. Sprinkle the brioche mixture over them and bake for about 30 minutes. Serve cold with cinnamon cream.

Cinnamon Cream

300ml (½ pint) whipping cream
1 tbsp icing sugar
1 tsp ground cinnamon

Lightly whip the cream and fold in the dry ingredients. Chill before serving.

A good polish for Squire Lawson-Hope's leather riding boots:
use equal quantities of methylated spirits, vinegar and boiled linseed oil.
Shake before use

Peggy and Jack returned from Meyruelle on their first town-twinning visit with this recipe personally handwritten by Madame Beguet, one of the French delegation. It can be made with peaches, apricots, or apples, too – least that's what Mum thought she said.

BON APPETIT

Tarte aux Poires

INGREDIENTS

90g de beurre non salé
90g de sucre, et 15g pour la garniture
2 oeufs
15ml de Calvados or Armagnac
100g de poudre d'amandes
25g de farine tamisée
4 poires
15ml de jus du citron

Serves 6–8

Ingredients

90g (3½oz) butter
90g (3½oz) caster sugar, plus 1 tbsp for the topping
2 eggs
1 tbsp Calvados or brandy
100g (3½oz) ground almonds
25g (1oz) plain flour, sifted
4 large pears, peeled, cored and sliced
1 tbsp lemon juice

For the pastry:
225g (8oz) plain flour
1 tbsp icing sugar
150g (5oz) butter, diced
1 egg yolk
1 tbsp iced water

To make the pastry, sift the flour and icing sugar into a mixing bowl and then rub in the butter until the mixture resembles breadcrumbs. Make a well in the centre and add the egg yolk mixed with the water. Combine the ingredients with a fork, knead briefly to form a dough and then wrap in cling film and chill for 30 minutes. Roll out and use to line a 25cm (10in) loose-bottomed flan tin. Preheat the oven to 200°C/400°F/Gas 6.

For the filling, cream the butter and sugar together until light and fluffy, then beat in the eggs and Calvados or brandy. Fold in the ground almonds and sifted flour. Spread two-thirds of this mixture in the pastry case. Place the pear slices in a circular pattern on top and use the remaining mixture to fill the gaps. Bake for 10 minutes, then lower the oven temperature to 160°C/325°F/Gas 3 and bake for a further 20 minutes. Sprinkle on the lemon juice and the tablespoon of caster sugar and return to the oven for another 10 minutes to caramelise the top. Serve hot or cold with crème fraîche or cream whipped together with a dash of Calvados.

Clarrie's Country Clanger

This is Clarrie's version of the sweet end of the traditional Borsetshire Clanger. Clarrie pops some soft fruit in with the jam to make it especially juicy, and Joe and Eddie can't wait to dig their spoons into this sweet, syrupy pud.

SERVES 8–10

225g (8oz) self-raising flour
pinch of salt
115g (4oz) vegetable suet, shredded
115g (4oz) caster sugar
grated zest of 1 orange
150ml (5fl oz) orange juice
90g (3½oz) apricot jam
225g (8oz) chopped cooking apple,
  raspberries and blackberries

Preheat the oven to 200°C/400°F/Gas 6. Sift the flour and salt together in a bowl, before adding the suet, sugar and orange zest. Mix thoroughly. Make a well in the centre and add the orange juice, then mix to form a soft dough. Turn onto a floured board and roll out to an oblong about 32 x 20cm (12½ x 8in). Spread the jam to within 2.5cm (1in) of the edges and sprinkle on the fresh fruit. Brush the edges with water and roll up the narrow end. Wrap in greaseproof paper and bake on a tray in the middle of the oven for 40 minutes.

Delicious served with syrup sauce.

Syrup Sauce

3 tbsp golden syrup
grated zest and juice of 1 lemon
175ml (6fl oz) water

Put all the ingredients in a pan and heat gently for 5–10 minutes, stirring constantly.

OCTOBER

1 MON PHEASANT SHOOTING BEGINS	**2** TUE	**3** WED	**4** THU *Borchester Mop Fair*	**5** FRI
7 SUN	**8** MON	**9** TUE	**10** WED	**11** THU
13 SAT	**14** SUN	**15** MON *Dan's birthday*	**16** TUE	**17** WED

AUTUMN COBBLER

1lb blackberries
5oz sugar
2 tbsp cornflour
1 tsp cinnamon
4oz butter or lard
6oz flour
3 tbsp milk

Toss the blackberries in 4oz of the sugar, the cornflour and cinnamon, and place in a buttered pie dish. Rub the lard lightly in to the flour and stir in the remaining sugar and milk. Roll out the paste to the size of the dish. Place on top of the fruit, trim the edges and prick with a fork. Bake in a hot oven for 30–40 minutes. Serve hot with custard.

23 TUE	**24** WED
26 FRI	**27** SAT
29 MON	**30** TUE

6
SAT

12
FRI

SAVOURY LIVER CASSEROLE

½lb onions, peeled
2 eating apples, peeled
½lb streaky bacon
1lb sheep's liver
breadcrumbs
mixed herbs
1 tsp Worcestershire sauce
stock

Chop the onions and apples and cut the bacon into thin strips. Wash the liver and cut into slices. Place a layer of liver in a casserole dish, cover with bacon, sprinkle with breadcrumbs, onion, apple and mixed herbs. Repeat these layers until the dish is full. Pour on the Worcestershire Sauce and enough stock to cover the meat. Put a lid on the pot and cook at 350ºF for 1½ hours.

| **18** THU | **19** FRI | **20** SAT *Tom's birthday* | **21** SUN | **22** MON |

25
THU

28
SUN

31
WED

OLD-FASHIONED WALNUT CAKE

¼lb shelled walnuts
¼lb butter or margarine
¼lb caster sugar
4 egg whites
3oz plain flour
½ tsp baking powder
pinch of salt

Toast the walnuts in the oven for a few minutes, then crush them. Cream the butter and sugar until light and fluffy. Beat the egg whites until fairly stiff, then stir them into the creamed butter alternately with the sifted flour, baking powder and salt. Fold in the walnuts. Pour the mixture into a greased and lined shallow sandwich tin. Bake at 350ºF for about an hour until the cake is browned and firm to touch.

The Carters' Chocolate Crunch Pie

Such a simple recipe so I've handed it on to Susan. She can impress the newly-weds if they drop by unexpectedly for Sunday lunch. 'Make it when you have time to spare, Susan, and pop it into the freezer', I suggested to her.

SERVES 12

350g (12oz) good-quality plain chocolate
175g (6oz) unsalted butter
55g (2oz) digestive biscuits, crushed
55g (2oz) ginger biscuits, crushed
55g (2oz) glacé pineapple, chopped
55g (2oz) glacé cherries, halved
55g (2oz) candied peel, chopped
55g (2oz) ready-to-eat dried apricots, chopped

Break up the chocolate and melt it with the butter in a large bowl set over a pan of simmering water, making sure the water is not touching the base of the bowl. Stir in the biscuits and chopped dried fruits. Spoon the mixture into a lined shallow 20cm (8in) round tin. Spread the mixture evenly, pressing down well, and cover with cling film or foil. Chill for several hours until firm. Cut into small slices to serve.

Doctor Locke's Dales Cake

Dr Locke was surprisingly easy to talk to despite his north country accent. He said that this recipe was a departure from his mother's traditional cheesecake, but I think it's really delicious – as delicious as he thought Debbie was for a time!

MAKES A 20CM (8IN) CAKE

175g (6oz) self-raising flour
1 tsp baking powder
75g (3oz) soft brown sugar
55g (2oz) raisins
55g (2oz) sultanas
55g (2oz) walnuts, chopped
2 eggs
90ml (3fl oz) vegetable oil
450g (1lb) cooking apples, cored, peeled
    and chopped
225g (8oz) Wensleydale cheese with
    apricot or Borsetshire cheese, crumbed

Preheat the oven to 180°C/350°F/Gas 4. Grease and line a deep 20cm (8in) loose-based cake tin. Sift the flour and baking powder into a bowl and stir in the sugar, raisins, sultanas and walnuts. Beat the eggs together with the oil and stir into the dry ingredients. Finally, add the chopped apples. Put half the mixture into the prepared tin, cover with the grated cheese and then top with the remaining cake mixture. Bake for 50–60 minutes, until the cake is shrinking from the sides of the tin. Leave to cool in the tin for 10 minutes, then turn out on a wire rack to cool completely.

Rosie's Yarmouth Biscuits

Clarrie's elder sister Rosie, tucked away in East Anglia, has proved to be a welcome 'port in a storm' for Clarrie on more than one occasion.

MAKES 45–50 BISCUITS

225g (8oz) butter
225g (8oz) caster sugar
3 eggs, beaten
350g (12oz) plain flour
175g (6oz) currants
½ tsp grated nutmeg

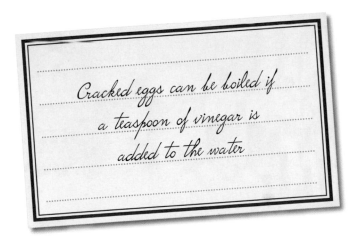

Preheat the oven to 190°C/375°F/Gas 5. Grease 2 baking sheets. Beat the butter and sugar together until soft and pale. Add all the remaining ingredients and stir together until the mixture forms a stiff dough. Place heaped teaspoonfuls of the mixture, well spaced out, on the baking sheets, lightly pressing them flat with the palm of your hand. Bake for 12–15 minutes, until golden brown around the edges, then transfer to a wire rack and leave to cool.

Cracked eggs can be boiled if a teaspoon of vinegar is added to the water

Auntie Pru's Cinnamon-spiced Apricots

Dear, gentle Auntie Pru's pantry was a veritable harvest festival – rows of colourful preserves, freshly-baked loaves and flat wire racks of cooling cakes. No wonder Uncle Tom was so portly, but who could resist her country fare? Uncle Tom's greatest delight was to tuck into a generous slice of cold gammon, a brown crusty roll and spiced apricots – all washed down with a mug of cider.

MAKES ABOUT 900G (2LB)

675g (1½lb) apricots
1 blade of mace
350ml (12fl oz) cider vinegar
175g (6oz) granulated sugar
cinnamon sticks, cut in half

Put the apricots in a large bowl, pour over boiling water to cover and leave for 1 minute. Take them out, plunge into cold water, then peel off the skins. Put the apricots, blade of mace, vinegar and sugar into a stainless steel pan and heat gently to dissolve the sugar. Bring to the boil and simmer for a few minutes until the apricots are just tender but still hold their shape. Remove the apricots with a slotted spoon and pack into sterilised jars, adding a piece of cinnamon stick to each jar. Boil the remaining syrup until it is thick, then pour it over the apricots so that they are completely covered. Seal immediately. Leave for at least a month before opening.

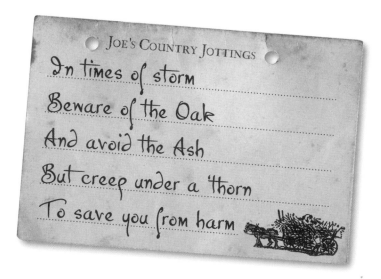

JOE'S COUNTRY JOTTINGS

In times of storm
Beware of the Oak
And avoid the Ash
But creep under a 'thorn
To save you from harm

The Feathers Borchester

POACHED EGGS ON TOAST

MUSHROOMS ON TOAST

HERRING ROE ON TOAST

WELSH RAREBIT

PORK PIE AND FARMHOUSE PICKLE

SELECTION OF PASTRIES

TEA

October 196

Tweedy and twilled local Borsetshire farmers were found on market days in the smoky Lounge Bar of The Feathers, faces florid from fresh air and the wood fire's glow. Only savoury, buttery mouthfuls punctuating their otherwise constant chatter. Then, comfortably replete and cloth caps replaced, back out into the busy street and down winding, muddy country lanes to home.

Uncle Walter's Walnut Biscuits

If old Uncle Walter wasn't pickling his walnuts he was asking Granny Perkins to use them in her baking. I think this recipe must have been hers.

MAKES 12 BISCUITS

150g (5oz) **plain flour**
pinch of salt
115g (4oz) **margarine (or butter if you can afford it)**
115g (4oz) **granulated sugar**
1 heaped tsp **coffee powder**
25g (1oz) **chopped walnuts**

Preheat the oven to 160°C/325°F/Gas 3. Sift the flour and salt into a bowl. Chop the margarine or butter into small lumps and rub it into the flour until it resembles breadcrumbs. Fork in the sugar, coffee and walnut pieces. Roll the mixture into walnut-sized balls and place, well spaced out, on a baking tray. Flatten them with a fork and bake for about 25–30 minutes until golden. Leave to cool before moving to a wire rack.

Never wash valuable china without first lining the basin with a soft, thick towel

Bring-and-Buy Brownies

- 115g (4oz) good-quality plain chocolate
- 115g (4oz) butter
- 225g (8oz) caster sugar
- ½ tsp vanilla essence
- 2 eggs, beaten
- 150g (5oz) self-raising flour
- 115g (4oz) walnuts, roughly chopped

Preheat the oven to 180°C/350°F/ Gas 4. Grease and line the base of a 18 x 28cm (7 x 11in) tin. Break up the chocolate and melt it in a large bowl set over a pan of hot water, making sure the water is not touching the base of the bowl. Cool slightly. Beat in the butter and sugar, then add the vanilla essence and eggs, a little at a time. Fold in the flour and chopped nuts. Turn the mixture into the tin and bake for 25–35 minutes, until the mixture is shrinking from the sides of the tin. Leave to cool in the tin, then cut into pieces. Store in an airtight tin or freeze immediately.

When you need help, ask a busy woman, they say, and that was Betty Tucker. Cakes for the cake stall, cleaning for the Snells, helping in the dairy, barmaiding at The Bull. She would never say no to anyone – except Brian, I believe!

Auntie Pru's tips for perfect pickles and jams

- Never use a copper or brass preserving pan for chutneys and pickles – it will give them a metallic taste.

- Use a stainless steel knife for chopping fruit and vegetables. Stir with a wooden spoon.

- Never make jam with over-ripe fruit.

- To sterilise jars and bottles, wash them in hot soapy water, rinse well and dry on a clean cloth, then place in a low oven. Fill the jars while hot.

- Pack down the preserves in the jars to remove air bubbles. Seal when the contents are piping hot or completely cold – never lukewarm. Dip the paper discs in brandy first if sealing cold.

- Always label and date the jars and store in a cool, dark, airy cupboard or shelf, larder or cellar.

- Most chutneys and jams improve if stored for 2–3 weeks before opening.

Mediterranean Quince Leather

As Elizabeth remembers, Julia harvested a trug of delicately-scented quinces from a somewhat overgrown tree at Lower Loxley Hall. Eager to demonstrate the richness of her experience in Spain, she chopped up the oddly shaped fruits and created a delicious paste to accompany a chunk of Manchego cheese. It can be eaten as a dessert, too, dredged with sifted icing sugar.

MAKES ABOUT 225G (8OZ)

900g (2lb) ripe quinces
juice of 1 lemon
450ml (15fl oz) water
granulated or preserving
**   sugar**

Wash and wipe the quinces to remove the downy coating, then chop them (no need to core and peel) and place in a pan with the lemon juice and water. Cover the pan and simmer for 30–40 minutes, until the quinces are soft. Liquidise the pulp, sieve it, then weigh the purée. Return the purée to the saucepan, stir in an equal weight of sugar and bring to the boil over a low heat, stirring to prevent sticking. Boil, stirring frequently, until the mixture becomes dry and thick. Spoon into a shallow container in a layer about 2.5cm (1in) thick, cover with a cloth and leave in a warm place to dry for a few days. Cut into squares and store in an airtight tin.

Martha's Mellow September Jelly

Old Martha Woodford liked nothing better on a melancholy autumn afternoon than shutting down the shop blinds and setting off on her bicycle along the narrow country lanes, hedges burgeoning with nature's bounty. She would return with her basket brimming-over with blackberries, crab apples, rosehips and rowanberries, 'God's gifts,' she'd call them, 'all for nothing, too. To make jam for my Joby's tea.'

MAKES 2–2.5KG (4–5LB)

1.1kg (2½lb) blackberries
1.1kg (2½lb) crab apples or cooking
   apples, chopped
2 lemons, sliced
1 cinnamon stick
4 cloves
1.2 litres (2 pints) water
granulated or preserving sugar

Pick over the blackberries, rinse them and place in a preserving pan. Add the apples, lemon slices, cinnamon stick and cloves. Pour in the water and simmer gently until the fruit is very soft, crushing it from time to time with the back of the spoon.

Put the fruit in a jelly bag and leave it to drip for at least 2 hours or overnight. Measure the juice, then return it to the pan, adding 450g (1lb) sugar for every 600ml (1 pint) of juice. Heat gently, stirring until the sugar has dissolved, then bring to the boil and boil rapidly until setting point has been reached: to test for this, put a teaspoonful of the jelly on a saucer, place in the fridge for a minute or two and then gently push the jelly with your finger – if it wrinkles it is ready. Skim off any scum, pour into sterilised jars and seal while hot.

Doris's Dumpsie Dearie Jam

'My! That smells good Doris!' Dan would say as he scrubbed the soil off his hardworking hands under the scullery tap. It was one of his favourite dinners – we call it Borsetshire Clanger. One end of the steamed roly-poly suet pudding oozed with this sweet orchard jam, the other was stuffed with rich mince and gravy. It was an easy way of cooking a complete meal in a muslin cloth over a steaming copper pan.

INGREDIENTS

- 1.1kg (2½lb) large plums
- 1 cinnamon stick
- 1.1kg (2½lb) cooking apples
- 1.1kg (2½lb) ripe pears
- granulated sugar or preserving sugar
- juice of 1 lemon
- ½ tsp grated nutmeg, or to taste

MAKES ABOUT 3-4KG (6-8LB)

Stone and chop the plums, then tie the stones and cinnamon stick into a piece of muslin. Peel, core and slice the apples and pears. Weigh all the prepared fruit, then put it in a preserving pan, adding 450g (1lb) sugar for each 450g (1lb) fruit. Let it stand until the juices run, then add the lemon juice and nutmeg. Bring to the boil, stirring to dissolve the sugar. Add the muslin bag and boil rapidly for 15 minutes or until the setting point is reached: to test for this, put a teaspoonful of the jam on a saucer, place it in the fridge for a minute or two and then gently push it with your finger – if it wrinkles it is ready. Pour into sterilised jars and seal while hot.

Auntie Chris's Plum and Ginger Chutney

Sadly no George to enjoy Chris's spicy autumn chutney in his chunky cheese sandwiches, but she finds these frilly-topped jars make good cheap Christmas gifts and sell well on the WI stall.

MAKES ABOUT 2KG (4LB)

1kg (2½lb) plums, stoned and chopped
grated zest and juice of 2 oranges
225g (8oz) onions, peeled and chopped
225g (8oz) sultanas
1 tbsp finely chopped or grated root
   ginger
1 tsp ground cinnamon
2 tsp ground allspice
1 tsp ground cardamom
2 cloves
1 tsp salt
600ml (1 pint) red wine vinegar
225g (8oz) demerara sugar
115g (4oz) walnuts, chopped

Put all the ingredients into a preserving pan and bring to the boil, stirring. Reduce the heat and simmer for 1–1½ hours, stirring frequently until the relish is very thick and glossy. Ladle into sterilised jars and seal with vinegar-proof tops while very hot.

JOE'S COUNTRY JOTTINGS

Many haws in October
and blue black sloes
means many cold fingers
and very cold toes

Colonel Danby's Military Pickle

To combat the draughts and winter chill of Ambridge Hall, old Colonel Danby and his companion, Aunt Laura, kept themselves warm with woolly 'coms' and deliciously indigestible suppers of bubbling rarebit and spicy Military Pickle.

MAKES ABOUT 2KG (4LB)

225g (8oz) green tomatoes, chopped
2 large pickling cucumbers, diced
450g (1lb) cauliflower, broken into
   florets
450g (1lb) baby onions, peeled but left
   whole
450g (1lb) courgettes, sliced
225g (8oz) white cabbage, shredded
55g (2oz) nasturtium seeds (optional)
2 tbsp salt
2 tsp ground turmeric
1 tbsp mustard powder
2 tsp ground ginger
1 tbsp cornflour
1.2 litres (2 pints) white wine
   vinegar
1 tbsp black peppercorns
2 garlic cloves, finely chopped

Put all the vegetables in a bowl with the nasturtium seeds, if using, sprinkle with the salt, cover and leave overnight. The next day, rinse in a colander and drain well. Mix the turmeric, mustard and ginger with the cornflour and a little of the vinegar to a smooth paste. Put it into a saucepan, with the remaining vinegar, the peppercorns and garlic. Simmer for 15 minutes, stirring, until the sauce thickens. Pack the vegetables into sterilised jars and pour on the mustard sauce. Seal with vinegar-proof tops while hot.

Always store pickles in glass – or stoneware

Al Clancy's Spicy Salsa

Charming, drawling Americans, Al and Mary-Jo Clancy, doing a house swap with Lynda and Robert Snell some years back, left a few handy hints on the pinboard at Ambridge Hall – much more useful than that frightful warming loo seat. 'Scoop up the salsa with crackers or corn-chips,' scribbled Al, and I'll have a salty Margarita with it. Enjoy it guys!

This is a cross between a sauce and a relish, depending on how finely you chop the ingredients.

SERVES 4

1 red onion, peeled
4 large, ripe tomatoes, skinned
2 chillies
55g (2oz) coriander leaves
juice of 1 lime and 1 lemon
salt

Chop the onion and tomatoes into small dice. Remove the stems from the chillies, and the seeds if you wish, and chop the flesh finely. Chop the coriander leaves. Put the ingredients into a bowl and combine with the lime and lemon juice and salt to taste. Chill before serving.

NOVEMBER

1 THU	**2** FRI

FIRESIDE FRUIT LOAF

2oz butter or margarine
2oz lard
8oz self-raising flour
1 tsp mixed spice
2oz sugar
2 tbsp treacle
8oz mixed fruit (dried)
1oz candied peel, chopped
milk to mix

Rub the butter and lard into the flour and mixed spice. Add the sugar, treacle, mixed fruit and candied peel. Mix with the milk until stiff and put into a lined, greased 1lb loaf tin. Bake at 300ºF for about 2 hours.

8 THU	**9** FRI
15 THU	**16** FRI

22 THU	**23** FRI	**24** SAT	**25** SUN	**26** MON

POTTED PIGEON

3 plump pigeons, skinned and cleaned
salt and pepper
1 tbsp brown sauce
melted butter

Place the pigeons in a pan of boiling water and simmer until the meat is tender and coming away from the bones. Mince the meat finely. Reduce the cooking stock, add the seasoning and brown sauce. Add some of the stock to the minced meat to moisten. Pack into sterile jars and top with a little melted butter. When cold, cover and seal.

28 WED

30 FRI

3 SAT	4 SUN	5 MON	6 TUE	7 WED
10 SAT	11 SUN ST. MARTIN'S DAY	12 MON	13 TUE *Peggy's birthday*	14 WED
17 SAT	18 SUN	19 MON	20 TUE	21 WED

27 TUE

29 THU

WEEKEND TREACLE PUDDING

4oz butter
4oz sugar
2 eggs, beaten
grated zest of 1 large orange
6oz self-raising flour
4 tbsp golden syrup

Grease a large 2-pint pudding basin and line the base with greaseproof paper. Beat together the butter, sugar, eggs and orange zest until soft, then fold in the flour. Spoon the syrup into the basin and cover with the sponge mixture. Cover the basin with greaseproof paper and steam for 1½–2 hours. Serve with hot custard.

WINTER

Winter is with us now – a fretwork of trees
in Lyttleton Cover etched filigree fashion
against the cold, grey, windswept sky. Bridge
Farm's organic vegetables stay earthbound and
silver-rimmed with the rime of frost. Inside
the flowery-curtained comfort of the cottages,
an amber glow and spicy warmth to greet us.
Floury crusty loaves sit proudly on the pine-
topped table with glossy currancy buns and
trays of crumbly biscuits. All the fare on a
typical cottager's baking day.

VENISON TERRINE

SERVES 8–10

450g (1lb) lean venison, minced

450g (1lb) lean pork or veal, minced

225g (8oz) lean bacon, or pancetta, chopped

1 tsp mixed peppercorns, crushed

2 tbsp onion, finely chopped

1 garlic clove, peeled and finely chopped

55g (2oz) button mushrooms, chopped

1 tsp chopped thyme

55g (2oz) fresh breadcrumbs

1 egg, beaten

Preheat the oven to 150°C/300°F/ Gas 2. Grease and line a 450g (1lb) loaf tin. In a large bowl, mix together the meat, then, with your hands, work in the pepper, onion, garlic, mushrooms, thyme and breadcrumbs. Add the beaten egg and combine the mixture well. Place in the loaf tin, pressing down to make sure that there are no air pockets, and cover with foil. Place in a roasting tin, adding water to the tin until it comes about halfway up the side of the loaf tin. Cook for 1½ hours.

Remove from the oven, then place weights on the top of the terrine and allow to chill overnight. Slice to serve.

Happily combining Home Farm venison and Tom's pork, this delicious meat loaf lends itself to a perfect winter picnic – sandwiched between thick slices of crusty country loaf. And it's even more delicious served with a generous dollop of Grundy's Fuggle Mustard (see p. 57) or redcurrant jelly.

49

Mary Pound's Cock-a-Leekie Pie

Clad in winter woollies and tucked away in a little brick bungalow in Edgeley, that was Ken's widow, Mary. Her gravelly voice could be heard grumbling over the fence. One of life's losers, in a way.

SERVES 4–6

1 onion, peeled and sliced
2 leeks, trimmed and sliced
225g (8oz) cooked chicken, diced
2 hard boiled eggs, halved
2 eggs, beaten
150ml (5fl oz) milk
grated nutmeg
salt and pepper

For the pastry:
225g (8oz) plain flour
pinch of salt
55g (2oz) hard margarine, diced
55g (2oz) lard or vegetable fat, diced
225g (8oz) mashed potatoes

To make the pastry, sift the flour and salt into a bowl, then rub in the margarine and lard or vegetable fat until the mixture resembles breadcrumbs. Add the mashed potatoes and mix to a pliable dough. Wrap in cling film and chill for 30 minutes, then roll out the pastry and use half of it to line a 20cm (8in) pie plate.

Preheat the oven to 200°C/400°F/Gas 6. Cook the onions and leeks in boiling salted water for 3–4 minutes, then drain thoroughly and layer them in the pie dish with the chicken and hard-boiled eggs, seasoning well between layers. Whisk the beaten eggs into the milk, season with nutmeg, salt and pepper and pour over the filling. Roll out the remaining potato pastry and use to cover the pie, pressing the edges together to seal. Make air vents in the top of the pie with a knife, brush with milk and bake for 30–40 minutes or until the pastry is golden and the filling set.

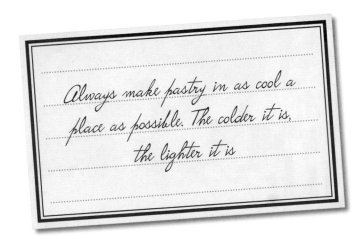

Always make pastry in as cool a place as possible. The colder it is, the lighter it is

Bert's Potager's Pot

Tripping over a trug of muddy, earthy vegetables grown by my wonderful son-in-law, Ian, I decided to peel, scrub and make use of them right away with a recipe given to me years ago by dear old Bert Fry. What could be more delicious on a misty, frosty day?

SERVES 8–10

2 tbsp olive oil
3 large onions, peeled and chopped
450g (1lb) waxy potatoes, peeled and diced
225g (8oz) carrots, peeled and sliced
1 celeriac, peeled and chopped into 2.5cm (1in) chunks
225g (8oz) parsnips, peeled and chopped into 2.5cm (1in) chunks
450ml (15fl oz) vegetable stock
2 bay leaves
salt and pepper

Heat the oil in a flameproof casserole. Sauté the onions until transparent over a moderate heat. Stir in the potatoes, carrots, celeriac and parsnips and cook over a low heat for 5–10 minutes. Add the stock, bay leaves and seasoning. Cover and simmer over a low heat for 40 minutes. You can discard the bay leaves at any time. I leave this to cook slowly in the bottom oven (not hotter than 150°C/300°F/Gas 2) until Brian and Adam come in from the fields, and serve it with wholemeal bread and a good chunk of mature Cheddar cheese.

Comforting Celebration Casserole

Having bought the pork from nephew Tom, Lilian cooked this casserole in a very slow oven ready for Matt's return!

SERVES 6

4 tbsp olive oil
700g (1½lb) boneless leg of pork, cut into 2.5cm (1in) chunks
2 large onions, peeled and sliced
2 garlic cloves, peeled and chopped
170g (6oz) ready-to-eat dried apricots, halved
2 tbsp ground coriander
1 tbsp ground cumin
1 tbsp ground cinnamon
2 tbsp plain flour
450ml (15fl oz) chicken stock or bouillon cube
grated zest and juice of 1 large orange
salt and pepper

Preheat the oven to 150°C/300°F/Gas 2. Heat the oil in a shallow frying pan and brown the meat in small batches. Drain on kitchen paper. In a flameproof casserole, gently fry the onions and garlic until soft, then add the apricots and spices and sauté gently. Stir in the flour and gradually add the stock, orange zest and juice. Season with salt and pepper. Bring to the boil and add the meat. Cover and cook for 2 hours until the meat is tender.

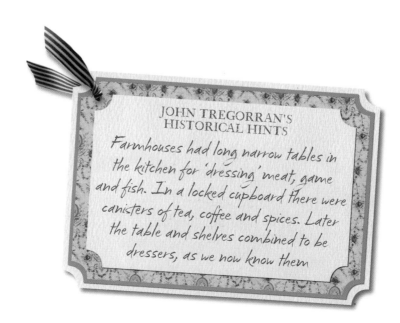

JOHN TREGORRAN'S HISTORICAL HINTS

Farmhouses had long narrow tables in the kitchen for 'dressing' meat, game and fish. In a locked cupboard there were canisters of tea, coffee and spices. Later the table and shelves combined to be dressers, as we now know them

Ham and Veal Shooting-party Pocket-sized Pies

Not to be outdone by nephew Tom chatting to him about big veal and ham pies, Brian suggested a mini version to soften up his corporate clients on a chilly winter's shoot.

MAKES 8 INDIVIDUAL PIES

1 tbsp sunflower oil
1 onion, peeled and finely
   chopped
225g (8oz) lean pie veal, trimmed
   and diced
225g (8oz) lean cooked ham,
   diced
1 tsp anchovy essence
1 tsp chopped thyme
1 tsp chopped parsley
salt and pepper
1 egg, beaten, to glaze

For the hot water-crust pastry:
450g (1lb) plain flour
1 tsp salt
200g (7oz) lard
200ml (7fl oz) water

To make the pastry, sift the flour and salt together in a bowl. In a saucepan melt the lard in the water, bring to the boil and pour into the flour. Beat the mixture together and knead to form a soft dough. Divide the pastry into 8 pieces, and roll out to line 8 x 10cm (4in) diameter flan tins, leaving enough pastry for the lids. Roll out the remaining pastry and cut the lid pieces, and put to one side (it's important to work and use the pastry before the fat sets and it becomes hard and flaky).

To make the filling, heat the oil in a flameproof casserole and fry the onion until transparent and soft, then add the veal and fry until golden. Add the ham, anchovy essence and herbs, then season well. Cover and simmer gently for 10 minutes. Allow to cool. Preheat the oven to 180°C/350°F/Gas 4.

Spoon the cooled mixture into each tin and cover with the pastry lids, moistening the edges with a little water and pressing together firmly to seal. Brush with beaten egg, then pierce a hole in the centre of each pie to allow the steam to escape. Bake for 30–40 minutes until golden brown.

DECEMBER

1 SAT	**2** SUN	**3** MON	**4** TUE	**5** WED
8 SAT	**9** SUN	**10** MON GROUSE SEASON ENDS	**11** TUE	**12** WED

CAROL SINGERS' WARMING PARKIN

1½lb plain flour
1 tsp bicarbonate of soda
8oz dark brown sugar
1 tsp cinnamon
2 tsp ground ginger
8oz butter or margarine, melted
1½lb black treacle
4 eggs, beaten
a little milk

Mix all the dry ingredients together. Make a well in the centre and pour in the melted butter, treacle and eggs. Stir rapidly until smooth, adding a little milk if necessary. Pour into a greased and lined roasting tin and bake at 350°F for about 1½ hours. Store in an airtight tin.

15 SAT	**16** SUN
19 WED	**20** THU
26 WED *Borsetshire meet* BOXING DAY	**27** THU
29 SAT	**30** SUN

6 THU	**7** FRI	
13 THU	**14** FRI	
17 MON *Jack's Birthday*	**18** TUE	

ROAST CHRISTMAS CAPON

4oz pork

2oz veal

2oz chicken liver

½oz butter

2 slices stale bread, soaked in milk

1 large onion, peeled

1 large apple, peeled

1 tsp parsley, chopped

1 tsp thyme, chopped

1 tsp sage, chopped

1 egg yolk

3fl oz cider

salt and pepper

1 capon

Chop or mince the pork, veal and liver, and brown them in the butter in a heavy pan. Squeeze the excess milk from the bread. Chop or mince the onion and apple, and mix with the herbs. Mix all the ingredients with the egg yolk and a little of the cider. Season well. Stuff the cavity of the capon and roast in a hot oven, reducing the heat after 20 minutes. Cook for 15 minutes per lb, and baste regularly with the remaining cider.

21 FRI *Christine's Birthday*	**22** SAT	**23** SUN	**24** MON CHRISTMAS EVE	**25** TUE CHRISTMAS DAY

28 FRI	
31 MON	

APRICOT MINCEMEAT

1lb dried apricots

1lb dates

½lb currants

½lb raisins

1lb shredded beef suet

1 tsp mixed spice

1 cooking apple, peeled, cored and chopped

1lb brown sugar

1oz almonds, chopped

zest and juice of 1 orange

zest and juice of 1 lemon

Soak the apricots overnight, drain and chop. Stone the dates, currants and raisins. Mix all the ingredients together well, put into jars and store for at least two weeks.

Brookfield's Brandied Pineapple Mincemeat

Phil decided to surprise Jill with an exciting new epicurean delight. Donning his striped apron, he chopped and stirred one autumn afternoon and created this delicious sweetmeat. Sometime later he moved on to marmalade, and was just as successful.

MAKES 2.5KG (5LB)

225g (8oz) shredded suet
225g (8oz) raisins
225g (8oz) ready-to-eat dried apricots, finely chopped
225g (8oz) candied peel, finely chopped
225g (8oz) sultanas
225g (8oz) crystallised pineapple, finely chopped
225g (8oz) Cox's apples, grated (include the peel)
115g (4oz) blanched almonds, chopped
115g (4oz) glacé cherries, halved
450g (1lb) muscovado sugar
½ tsp ground mace
½ tsp ground cinnamon
½ tsp ground cloves
grated zest and juice of 2 lemons and 1 orange
300ml (½ pint) brandy

Mix all the ingredients together thoroughly in a large bowl. Cover with cling film and leave for 2 days in a cool place, stirring occasionally. Stir the mincemeat again very thoroughly and add more brandy if the mixture seems dry. Press into sterilised jars, seal and store for at least a month before using.

Grundy's Fuggle Mustard

A hot and spicy mustard guaranteed to start old Joe coughing and spluttering – but he can soon cool his throat with the remains of the Shires Best Bitter.

MAKES 1 SMALL POT

55g (2oz) black mustard seeds
55g (2oz) white mustard seeds
½ tsp black peppercorns
1 tsp ground mace
½ tsp grated horseradish
125ml (4fl oz) Shires Best Bitter

Crush the mustard seeds and peppercorns in a coffee grinder or pestle and mortar; they should be fairly finely crushed but still keep a bit of texture. Mix in a pan with all the other ingredients and warm over a low heat until a creamy paste is formed. Pour into a clean jar or earthenware pot and seal. Keep for 1 week before using.

Bert's Best Tips:
If there's frost in December,
take this for a law,
care for your strawberries
and cover with straw

Cameron Fraser's Tartan Marmalade

Leaving poor Elizabeth in the lurch, so cruelly too, Cameron's legacy to the village was his excellent Scottish recipe for tangy marmalade. I must say it's good, but that's more than could be said about Cameron.

MAKES ABOUT 2.5KG (5LB)

3 grapefruits
3 sweet oranges
3 lemons
2.4 litres (64fl oz) water
1.5kg (3lb) granulated sugar or preserving sugar
4 tbsp whisky

Wash and dry the fruit. Squeeze the juice, then remove the flesh and pips and tie them in a square of muslin. Finely slice the peel. Place the juice, peel and muslin bag in a preserving pan and add the water. Bring to the boil and simmer for about 2 hours, until the peel is really soft. Remove the muslin bag, then add the sugar and whisky and stir over a low heat until the sugar has dissolved. Boil rapidly until setting point is reached: to test for this, put a teaspoonful of the mixture on a saucer, place in the fridge for a minute or two and then gently push it with your finger – if it wrinkles it is ready. Skim, leave to cool for 30–45 minutes, then stir to distribute the peel evenly. Pour into sterilised jars and leave until completely cold, then seal.

Auntie Chris's Christmas Relish

A succulent clove-studded slab of gammon, a baked potato and a generous spoonful of Auntie Chris's Christmas relish was just the thing for an easy meal after exercising the horses. 'Ee – that were champion,' admitted George, loosening the buckle on his belt. 'I couldn't play one single note on my cornet now, not if you begged me.'

'Thank goodness for that,' Chris whispered under her breath.

MAKES ABOUT 225ML (8FL OZ)

2 shallots, peeled and finely chopped
grated zest of 1 orange
grated zest of 1 lemon
4 tbsp redcurrant jelly
½ tsp mustard powder
½ tsp ground ginger
150ml (5fl oz) port
1 tsp red wine vinegar
salt and pepper

Put the shallots in a small pan of boiling water, simmer for a minute or two, then drain. Finely pare the zest from the orange and lemon and cut into very thin shreds. Blanch the zest in boiling water for 1 minute, then drain. Melt the redcurrant jelly in a saucepan, stir in the mustard and ginger, then add the shallots, citrus zest, port and wine vinegar. Season with salt and pepper. Bring to the boil and simmer for 5–10 minutes, until the sauce thickens. Remove from the heat and leave to cool completely, before covering and refrigerating. Serve chilled. It should keep in the fridge for about 2 weeks.

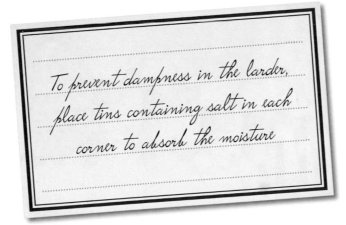

To prevent dampness in the larder, place tins containing salt in each corner to absorb the moisture

Country Park Chestnuts in Brandy

Whether or not the wild sweet chestnuts growing handsomely in the Country Park are plump enough to make the harvesting worthwhile, this is a good recipe to have tucked away in the drawer – after all, it's easy enough to buy a bag of the glossy brown nuts from the market in Borchester.

MAKES ABOUT 900G (2LB)

450g (1lb) fresh chestnuts
675g (1½lb) granulated sugar
600ml (1 pint) water
juice of 2 lemons
90ml (3fl oz) brandy

Slit the chestnut skins with a sharp knife and cook them in a pan of boiling water until just tender. Drain and peel carefully, removing the brown inner skin.

Put the sugar, water and lemon juice in a pan and boil to a thick syrup. Add the cooked chestnuts to the syrup and simmer for 10 minutes. Remove from the heat, cover and leave to stand for 24 hours. The next day reheat the mixture and boil for 5 minutes. The syrup should have a thick, honeyed consistency. Add the brandy, stirring it in carefully. Pour into sterilised jars and seal while hot.

JOHN TREGORRAN'S
HISTORICAL HINTS

Sugar was bought in a block and had to be scraped with a sharp knife

Saddler's Tea Rooms
Borchester

Toasted teacakes

Mince pies

Scone, butter and homemade jam

Iced fancies

India or China tea

Dec 197

On a bag-bulging, boot-pinching, back-breaking Borchester shopping day Jill and I escape the busy High Street to the traditional tables of Saddler's Tea Rooms. Colourful lights wink and blink at us through bottle-glass panes as we each sink onto the cushioned comfort of a wheelback chair. Dainty doilies frame fondant-iced fancies, and a dusting of sugar frosts mince pies like powdered snow. This an oasis of calm on our Christmas shopping day.

Beaters' Broth

I've concocted this warming broth to keep the beaters happy on a frosty day's shoot. The guns are also partial to it, and I'm sure I noticed Brian tipping an extra bit of oomph into it from his hip flask. Naughty!

SERVES 8

2 tbsp olive oil

1 large Spanish onion, peeled and chopped

2 carrots, peeled and diced

2 garlic cloves, peeled and chopped

2 parsnips, peeled and diced

2 celery sticks, diced

1 litre (2 pints) beef consommé, thinned

125ml (4fl oz) red wine

salt and pepper

Heat the oil in a large pan and add the onion, carrots, garlic, parsnips and celery. Sauté over a low heat for about half an hour, until they are tender. Add the consommé, bring it to the boil and reduce the heat. Cover and simmer gently for 20 minutes.

Pour the broth into a liquidiser and blend with the red wine. Season well, then pour into flasks and take to the shoot picnic.

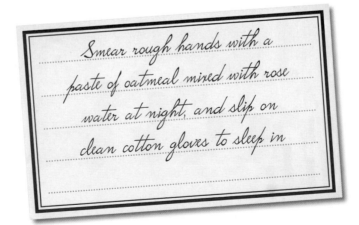

Smear rough hands with a paste of oatmeal mixed with rose water at night, and slip on clean cotton gloves to sleep in

Guns and Beaters' Warming Spice Cake

There are no old-fashioned hay-boxes lined with straw on the Home Farm shoot these days. Instead a flask or two of steaming-hot coffee, a snifter of brandy and some hefty chunks of wholesome fruit cake to keep out the cold on those damp December days. But after the pale winter sun sinks, and the 4x4s return down the bumpy, muddied tracks, it's time for laughter, baked potatoes and gravy-rich casserole in the warm and dry.

MAKES A 25CM (10IN) CAKE

450g (1lb) mixed dried fruit
300ml (¾ pint/12fl oz) Shires Best Bitter
225g (8oz) butter
225g (8oz) muscovado sugar
3 eggs
175g (6oz) wholemeal flour
175g (6oz) self-raising flour
1 tsp bicarbonate of soda
1 tsp mixed spice
1 tsp ground cinnamon
1 tsp ground ginger
115g (4oz) walnuts, chopped

Soak the mixed fruit in the beer overnight. The next day, preheat the oven to 160°C/325°F/Gas 3. Grease and line a 25cm (10in) round cake tin. Drain the fruit, reserving the beer. Cream the butter and sugar together until light and fluffy, then beat in the eggs with some of the drained beer. Sift together the flours, bicarbonate of soda and spices and fold them into the mixture. Add the dried fruit, walnuts and remaining beer and stir thoroughly, the mixture should have a soft dropping consistency. Spoon into the prepared tin and bake for 2½–3 hours, until a skewer inserted in the centre comes out clean. Leave to cool in the tin, then turn out the cake and store in an airtight container for a few days before cutting.

Uncle Walter's Warming Winter Elderberry Cordial

Granny Perkins simmered and stirred Uncle Walter's homemade brew, gossiping over the copper pan round at Honeysuckle Cottage.

MAKES ABOUT 600ML (1 PINT)

450g (1lb) ripe elderberries
450g (1lb) caster sugar
strip of orange zest

Place the elderberries in a large saucepan with the sugar and orange zest. Bring to the boil slowly, squashing the berries with a wooden spoon, then simmer for an hour, stirring occasionally. Strain through a muslin cloth, then bottle and seal.

To make a warming winter cordial, mull with a cinnamon stick, brown sugar and a twist of orange zest. Or dilute with spring water for a cool, refreshing summer drink.

63

My Splendidly Rich Mocha Truffles

My darling granddaughter Phoebe used to love putting on her pinafore and rolling the chocolatey balls with her capable little hands. She will never be too old to scrape out the bowl afterwards though!

MAKES 24

125ml (4fl oz) double cream
225g (8oz) good-quality plain chocolate, broken into small pieces
2 tbsp coffee-flavoured liqueur, such as Tia Maria
a few drops of coffee flavouring
3 tbsp cocoa powder

Pour the cream into a small heavy-based saucepan and bring to boiling point, stirring occasionally. Remove from the heat and carefully stir in the chocolate pieces until they have melted. Let the mixture cool a little and then stir in the liqueur and coffee flavouring. Put in the fridge and leave to set.

Sift the cocoa powder on to a plate. Take small spoonfuls of the paste, roll them into balls in the palms of your hands and then roll them in the cocoa, coating them well. Place on a sheet of greaseproof paper and chill. Keep refrigerated as much as possible.

Mrs Horrobin's Humbugs

I used to describe the Horrobins as humbugs, but of course now the commendable Carters are the exception.

MAKES ABOUT 450G (1LB)

450g (1lb) granulated sugar
3 drops of peppermint oil
150ml (5fl oz) water
1 tbsp golden syrup
pinch of cream of tartar

Put the sugar, peppermint oil and water into a large, heavy-based saucepan and heat gently until the sugar has dissolved. Stir in the golden syrup and the cream of tartar and bring slowly to boiling point. Boil until it reaches 149–154°C (300–310°F) on a sugar thermometer, then test by dropping a little of the mixture into cold water, it should form hard threads. Remove from the heat and cool a little, then pour on to an oiled slab. Using oiled knives, fold the ends of the toffee to the centre. When the toffee is cool enough to handle, pull it into strips, twist and chop them into humbug shapes. Leave on waxed paper to cool completely.

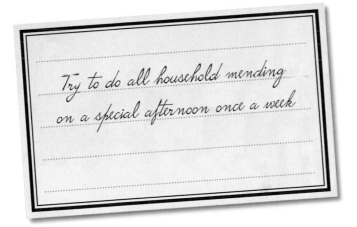

Try to do all household mending on a special afternoon once a week

Jim Lloyd's Ginger Candy

Away from his encyclopedias one afternoon, Jim decides to turn his hand to a singularly non-cerebral skill. 'Aaah, ginger. Did the Ancient Romans use ginger?' As the creamy mixture bubbled on the stove, his sticky fingers turned the well-thumbed pages once again.

MAKES ABOUT 1.1KG (2LB)

900g (2lb) granulated sugar
400ml (14fl oz) single cream
115g (4oz) preserved ginger in syrup,
   chopped

Gently heat the sugar and cream in a large heavy-based pan until the sugar has dissolved. Bring gradually to the boil, stirring constantly, and simmer for a few minutes until the mixture turns golden brown and reaches the stage when a soft ball forms when a teaspoonful is dropped into cold water. Remove from the heat and stir in the chopped ginger, then beat until it looks sugary. Pour into a well-greased tin in a layer about 2.5cm (1in) thick. When partially cool, mark into squares.

Manorfield Close's Moreish Mint Jellies

A haze of peppermint floats around the winter-woolly-clad mainstays of Manorfield Close as they cluster at the bus stop on Borchester Market Day.

MAKES 48

25g (1oz) gelatine
300ml (½ pint) water
450g (1lb) granulated sugar
1–2 drops of green food colouring
75ml (2½fl oz) crème de menthe, or 1 tbsp peppermint flavouring
55g (2oz) icing sugar, sifted

Sprinkle the gelatine over the water in a saucepan and leave in a warm place to dissolve. Add the sugar and heat gently until dissolved. Bring to the boil and simmer gently for about 10 minutes, skimming the white scum from the surface. Remove from the heat, cool slightly then add the food colouring and the crème de menthe or peppermint flavouring. Stir carefully, then pour into a dampened shallow 20cm (8in) square tin and leave in a cool place to set. Cut into squares and coat in the icing sugar.

Adam's Birthday Kisses

These were special favourites of dear little Adam when we lived over the bookshop in Borchester.

25g (1oz) unsalted butter
25g (1oz) caster sugar
1 egg
55g (2oz) plain flour
1 heaped tsp cocoa powder
½ tsp baking powder

For the icing:
25g (1oz) butter
55g (2oz) icing sugar
1tsp coffee esssence

Preheat the oven to 180°C/350°F/Gas 4. Cream together the butter and sugar, then add the egg and beat well. Sift in the flour, cocoa and baking powder. Drop a teaspoon of the mixture onto a greased baking tray and bake for 10 minutes. Remove from the oven and allow to cool completely. To make the icing, simply combine all of the ingredients and mix well. Use as a filling to sandwich two biscuits together.

HOME FARM, AMBRIDGE, BORSETSHIRE

Kathy Perks' Christmas Pudding Ice Cream

This was a great Christmas favourite on the Hassett Room's menu in Sid and Kathy's time at The Bull. After plates brimming with succulent roast turkey and scrumptious trimmings, some people preferred this cold dessert to the traditional Christmas pudding. And it's still full of seasonal spirit.

SERVES 10

225g (8oz) mixed dried fruit
55g (2oz) glacé cherries, halved
55g (2oz) ready-to-eat dried apricots, chopped
75ml (2½fl oz) brandy
3 eggs
2 egg yolks
125g (4½oz) caster sugar
300ml (½ pint) single cream
250ml (8fl oz) double cream
225g (8oz) fresh pineapple flesh

Put the mixed fruit, glacé cherries and dried apricots into a bowl and pour over the brandy. Leave to soak for 2–3 hours. Beat the eggs, egg yolks and sugar together until light and frothy. Heat the single cream to boiling and whisk it well into the egg mixture. Pour back into the pan and heat gently, stirring, until the custard thickens. Set aside to cool.

Lightly whip the double cream, fold it into the custard and then fold in the dried fruit and brandy mixture. Purée the fresh pineapple in a liquidiser and stir in to the mixture. Turn into a large bowl and freeze until firm. Transfer to the fridge 20 minutes before serving.

Alice's Favourite Fudge Spread

Even as a grown-up, newly-married young lady Alice will always be the apple of my eye – and this will always be her favourite treat.

This is an amazingly versatile chocolate fudge spread. Melt it as a fondue and dip fresh fruit in it. Warm it up for a runny sauce to pour over ice cream, or make chocolate and banana sandwiches. Yummy!

MAKES ABOUT 675G (1½LB)

115g (4oz) good-quality plain chocolate
115g (4oz) good-quality milk chocolate
115g (4oz) unsalted butter
175ml can of evaporated milk
115g (4oz) granulated sugar
2 tsp vanilla essence
90ml (3fl oz) double cream

Break up the chocolate and put in a heavy-based saucepan with the butter, evaporated milk, sugar and vanilla essence. Heat gently until the sugar has dissolved and the chocolate and butter have melted. Pour in the cream and bring to the boil, stirring constantly. Cool a little, then pour into sterilised jars and seal. Store in the fridge.

JOHN TREGORRAN'S
HISTORICAL HINTS

In grand houses sweetmeats
and delicate puddings were
made and set in fancy moulds
in a cool still room

Bored with being indoors on wet, wintry days, I packed up a picnic so Ben and Phoebe could join Ruairi on the hay bales in the barn for a fun-day, Sunday lunch. Ruairi thinks these are quite cool with olives and anchovies, but Ben's not so sure.

WINTER PICNIC PIZZAS

Serves 6

- ❏ 1 CIABATTA LOAF
- ❏ BUTTER FOR SPREADING
- ❏ 4 TBSP TOMATO KETCHUP
- ❏ 1 TIN OF TUNA FISH
- ❏ 8 ANCHOVY FILLETS
- ❏ 4OZ EMMENTHAL CHEESE, THINLY SLICED
- ❏ A SCATTERING OF BLACK OLIVES

SPLIT THE CIABATTA LOAF AND TOAST LIGHTLY ON THE INSIDE, THEN SPREAD THE INSIDES WITH BUTTER AND KETCHUP. DRAIN AND FLAKE THE TUNA, AND MOUND ON TOP OF THE BREAD. TOP WITH THE ANCHOVY FILLETS, THE CHEESE AND FINALLY THE OLIVES. GRILL UNTIL THE CHEESE MELTS.

PACK LOOSELY IN FOIL, KEEPING THE SLICES FLAT IN A TIN.

ROLY-POLY PORK SAUSAGES

Serves 6

- ❏ 6OZ FRESH BREADCRUMBS
- ❏ 1OZ GRATED PECORINO CHEESE
- ❏ 1LB SAUSAGEMEAT
- ❏ 1 LARGE BRAMLEY APPLE, PEELED, CORED AND FINELY CHOPPED OR GRATED
- ❏ 1 ONION, PEELED AND ROUGHLY CHOPPED
- ❏ 4OZ READY-TO-EAT DRIED APRICOTS, CHOPPED
- ❏ 3 OR 4 SAGE LEAVES, FINELY SNIPPED
- ❏ 2 TSP WHOLEGRAIN MUSTARD
- ❏ SALT AND PEPPER
- ❏ DASH OF WORCESTERSHIRE SAUCE
- ❏ 2OZ PLAIN FLOUR
- ❏ 1 EGG, BEATEN

PREHEAT THE OVEN TO 180°C/375°F/GAS 4. MEASURE 4OZ OF BREADCRUMBS AND MIX WITH THE PECORINO CHEESE. MIX TOGETHER THE SAUSAGEMEAT, APPLE, ONION AND APRICOTS, ADDING THE SAGE, MUSTARD, PLAIN BREADCRUMBS AND SEASONING AS YOU GO (YOU CAN DO THIS BY HAND OR IN A FOOD PROCESSOR) WITH SALT AND PEPPER AND THE WORCESTERSHIRE SAUCE. WASH AND DRY YOUR HANDS, AND THEN FORM THE MIXTURE INTO SAUSAGE SHAPES. ROLL THESE FIRST IN THE FLOUR, BEFORE DIPPING INTO THE EGG AND COATING THEM IN THE CHEESY BREADCRUMBS.

PLACE ON A BAKING TIN AND BAKE IN A PREHEATED OVEN FOR 30–40 MINUTES.

BUTTERY OAT SQUARES

SERVES 6–8

- 3½oz butter
- 3½oz demerara sugar
- 5oz rolled oats or porridge oats
- ½ tsp almond extract

Preheat the oven to 190°C/375°F/GAS 5. Grease a shallow baking tin. Put the butter in a saucepan and warm it over a low heat until it's melted. Stir the sugar, oats and almond essence into the melted butter and carefully tip the mixture into the baking tin. Press it down evenly with a wooden spoon. Bake in the oven on a middle shelf until a golden colour (about 20 minutes). Remove from the oven, and mark it into squares before completely cool.

I found this recipe in one of little Lilian's comics from many moons ago. One dull and drizzly afternoon, when all I could hear was squabbling, I bundled Ben and Ruairi into the kitchen, handed them a wooden spoon apiece, and lo and behold, after stirring and scraping and squashing and tasting, we all enjoyed a scrummy teatime treat!

PLEASE JOIN US FOR A

CHRISTMAS EVE SUPPER

AT HOME FARM

AFTER THE CAROL SERVICE

EVA'S GLÜHWEIN

·

CAROL'S CHRISTMAS SAVOURY ROULADE

ROASTED VEGETABLE AND GOAT'S CHEESE TARTLETS

PAT'S HOT POTATO AND PANCETTA SALAD

CHICORY, CELERIAC AND WALNUT SALAD

·

MINCEMEAT AND MERINGUE PIE

·

POTTED STILTON WITH PORT

As the bells of St Stephen's ring out in the frosty air, logs glow and crackle in the hearth at Home Farm.

A festive table, holly-sprigged and bauble-spangled, is laid with a generous Christmas supper's spread. 'Jenny darling, how you spoil us all', mumbled Brian – tucking into a succulent slice of savoury roulade.

Eva's Glühwein

There was much metaphorical thigh slapping when Eva Lenz, our au pair, left to marry local bobby Jim Coverdale. Brian drew the line at lederhosen and his chateau-bottled clarets when the German Lenzs came over for the wedding.

SERVES 12

3 bottles of cheap red wine
75g (3oz) caster sugar
2 cinnamon sticks, halved
juice of 1 orange and 1 lemon
12 cloves

Pour the wine into a large saucepan. Add the rest of the ingredients and heat gently, stirring to dissolve the sugar. Do not allow it to boil. Serve in glasses or mugs.

I discovered this hand-scribbled recipe only the other day when it fell out of a copy of 'Elizabethan Ballads' given to me years ago by my dear friend John Tregorran.
Memories – how sweet they are.

Carol's Christmas Savoury Roulade

Serves 8

1 large pork fillet (350–450g/12–16oz)

4 chicken breast fillets (280g–350g/10–12oz)

2 tsp green peppercorns (bottled)

6 anchovy fillets in oil

25g (1oz) capers

a handful of chopped parsley

2 garlic cloves, peeled and chopped

115g (4oz) thinly sliced German or Italian salami

olive oil

salt and pepper

Preheat the oven to 150°C/300°F/Gas 2. Butterfly the pork fillet by slicing it lengthways without cutting it right through, then lay it out on paper and flatten it by beating it with a meat hammer or rolling pin. Flatten the chicken fillets in the same way. Chop the peppercorns, anchovy fillets and capers, and mix together with the parsley and garlic, with a little bit of the anchovy oil to keep it loose. Spread some of the mixture onto the pork fillet, then cover with all of the chicken. Spread some more of the parsley mixture over and lay the salami slices on top. Spread the remains of the mixture onto the salami to cover. Now roll up the meat as you would a sponge roulade.

Place your roulade, seam-side-down, in a roasting tin. Rub with olive oil and season well. Wrap in foil and roast for 2 hours, removing the foil for the last half hour. Serve in slices, hot or cold, ideally with sweet cranberry and orange sauce.

Roasted Vegetable and Goat's Cheese Tartlets

Makes 8

1 red pepper, deseeded
half an aubergine
1 red onion, peeled and diced
olive oil
packet of shortcrust pastry
butter, for greasing
2 eggs

1 egg yolk
150ml (5fl oz) milk
150ml (5fl oz) double cream
150g (5oz) goat's cheese log
  (rind on)
salt and pepper

Preheat the oven to 150°C/300°F/Gas 2. Grease 8 x 10cm (4in) diameter, loose-bottomed, fluted tartlet tins. Chop the red pepper and aubergine into 1cm (½in) pieces, and mix with the onion. Put the vegetables into a roasting tray and drizzle with a little olive oil. Toss the vegetables to coat them, then put in the oven for about 30 minutes, turning occasionally so that they don't catch. When they are soft, remove from the oven and put to one side to cool slightly. Turn the oven temperature up to 180°C/350°F/Gas 4.

While the vegetables are cooking, roll out the pastry on a floured surface to 5mm thickness. Using a pastry cutter that is slightly larger than the tartlet tins, cut out the rounds of pastry. Press into the tartlet tins and refrigerate for 20 minutes, before baking blind until the pastry is golden. Beat the two eggs together, and use a little to brush the bottom of the tartlet cases to prevent them going soggy.

Add the egg yolk, milk and cream to the remaining beaten eggs, mix thoroughly, and then pass through a sieve into a jug. Season well. Scatter pieces of the roasted vegetables into each pastry case, and then pour over the egg mixture, being careful not to overfill the cases. Cut the goat's cheese into 5mm slices and lay a slice on the top of each of the tartlets. Bake in the middle of the oven for 15–20 minutes, until just set and the egg filling is golden. Remove from the oven and leave to cool in the tins for 5 minutes, before carefully turning out onto a wire rack to cool completely.

Chicory, Celeriac and Walnut Salad

SERVES 8

4 heads of chicory, rinsed
1 large celeriac, peeled and
    grated
a handful of chopped walnuts
bunch of spring onions, trimmed
    and sliced

For the dressing:
2 tbsp mayonnaise
1 tbsp walnut oil
1 tbsp lemon juice
2 tbsp plain yoghurt
salt and pepper

Place the chicory leaves around the base and sides of a salad bowl. Make the dressing my combining all of the ingredients well. Coat the celeriac, walnuts and onions in the dressing, and place in the centre of the chicory leaves.

Pat's Hot Potato and Pancetta Salad

SERVES 8

6 large waxy potatoes (Maris Peer
    are ideal)
1 tbsp shallots or red onion,
    peeled and finely diced
115g (4oz) pancetta or snipped
    streaky bacon
2 large pickled gherkins, chopped
juice of 1 lemon
1–2 tbsp mayonnaise
salt and pepper

Cook the potatoes whole in their skins in a pan of salted water. Drain well, and allow to cool slightly. Remove the skins with your fingers and dice, before covering with aluminium foil to keep warm. Next, gently fry the onion and pancetta over a gentle flame until the onion is translucent. In a large bowl, mix all of the ingredients together. Toss in the lemon juice and mayonnaise. Season to taste and serve immediately.

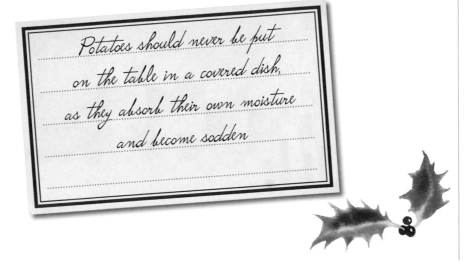

Potatoes should never be put
on the table in a covered dish,
as they absorb their own moisture
and become sodden

Mincemeat Meringue Pie

This is Ian's generous offering – jazzing up a traditional recipe

SERVES 8

15g (½oz) unsalted butter
2 egg yolks
1 tbsp brandy
225g (8oz) mincemeat
55g (2oz) glacé cherries, halved
25g (1oz) candied peel, chopped

For the pastry:
225g (8oz) plain flour
55g (2oz) caster sugar
150g (5oz) unsalted butter
1 egg yolk
3 tbsp cold water

For the meringue:
2 egg whites
115g (4oz) caster sugar

For the pastry, sift the flour into a bowl and, using your hands, mix with the sugar and butter. Add the egg yolk and mix gently, before adding the water to combine. Add the water gradually so that your pastry doesn't become too wet, and be careful not to over work it – although I would be inclined to buy it ready-made!

Thinly roll out the pastry and use to line a pie plate or tart tin. Leave to chill for 20 minutes, and preheat the oven to 190°C/375°F/Gas 5. Bake the pastry case blind until golden. Meanwhile, cream the butter, egg yolks and brandy and mix together with the mincemeat, cherries and candied peel. Fill the pastry case and bake at for 30 minutes. Remove from the oven and leave to rest while you make the meringue.

Whisk the egg whites until soft peaks appear then, still whisking, gradually add the sugar until the meringue is stiff and glossy. Top the tart with the meringue mixture and return to the oven for 20 minutes, or until the meringue is crisp and biscuit-coloured. Delicious served warm or cold, with cream or crème fraîche.

sauce in cocktails to give them a bit of Christmas flavour...'

Potted Stilton with Port

SERVES 6

225g (8oz) ripe Stilton
55g (2oz) butter, softened
2 tbsp port
1 garlic clove, peeled and crushed
125ml (4 fl oz) crème fraîche

Blend all the ingredients in a food processor to make a creamy mixture. Spoon into an airtight container and refrigerate until firm. Serve with crackers, rye bread and sticks of crispy celery.

Sweet Cranberry and Orange Sauce

225g (8oz) caster sugar
grated zest and juice of 1 orange
grated zest and juice of 1 lemon
175g (6oz) cranberries

Stir the sugar into the fruit juice in the pan, add the cranberries and simmer for 5 or 6 minutes. Store in the fridge for up to 2 weeks.

JOHN TREGORRAN'S HISTORICAL HINTS

Mince pies in Tudor Times were filled with minced beef or mutton, dried fruit and spices

KATE'S ALTERNATIVE CHRISTMAS DISHES

NUT & LENTIL ROAST
WITH RICH TOMATO SAUCE

•

ZESTY SWEET POTATO STUFFING

•

SPROUTS SUPREME
CREAMED CARROT AND MACE

•

GRAN'S RICH AND TRADITIONAL TRIFLE

Flipping through glossy pages in Underwood's stylish hair salon, I managed to find some excellent ideas for Kate's kind of vegetarian Christmas fare. I just couldn't wait to have her home again — at the time!

Zesty Sweet Potato Stuffing

Kate loved this and said it's a meal in itself.

SERVES 8–10

675g (1½lb) sweet potatoes,
   peeled and diced
2 tbsp olive oil
1 large carrot, peeled and diced
1 medium onion, peeled and diced
1 small leek, trimmed and thinly
   sliced
1 celery stick, diced
6 ready-to-eat dried apricots, diced
115g (4oz) walnuts, chopped
6 sage leaves, chopped
½ a small orange, grated zest and juice
salt and pepper

Cook the sweet potatoes in salted water for about 10 minutes until tender, then drain well and mash until smooth. Heat the oil in a saucepan and gently fry the carrot, onion, leek and celery until soft. Mix in the apricots, walnuts and sage. Add to the mashed sweet potatoes and season well. Either roll into balls, or scoop into a greased baking tin and smooth the top. Roast for about 40 minutes, until brown and crusty.

Nut & lentil roast

Serves 8-10

Preheat the oven to 190°C/375°F/Gas 5. Line a 450g (1lb) loaf tin with greaseproof paper. Rinse the lentils under cold running water, then add to a saucepan with the stock and bay leaf, and bring to the boil. Reduce the heat to a gentle simmer, then cover and cook, stirring occasionally, for 15 minutes until the lentils are soft and the stock has been absorbed. Discard the bay leaf.

Toast the cashew and pine nuts in a non-stick frying pan, stirring frequently. Set aside to cool, then roughly chop. You can use a food processor, but make sure they don't end up too finely ground.

Heat the oil in a heavy-based pan, and fry the onion, carrot and celery over a moderate heat for 5 minutes. Add the remaining vegetables to the pan and cook for a further 10–15 minutes, stirring occasionally, until tender. Add the lemon juice.

Mix the lentils and vegetables together in a large bowl. Stir in the breadcrumbs, nuts, parsley and oregano, followed by the grated cheese and beaten egg. Season to taste, then press into the loaf tin.

Cook for 30 minutes, then cover the top with foil to prevent it burning. Bake for a further 40 minutes, removing the foil again for the last 10 minutes – or until a skewer inserted comes out clean. Remove from the oven and leave to stand for 10 minutes before turning out and slicing at the table. Serve with tomato sauce.

- 200g (7½oz) red split lentils
- 500ml (16fl oz) vegetable stock
- 1 bay leaf
- 55g (2oz) unsalted cashew nuts
- 55g (2oz) pine nuts
- 2 tbsp olive oil
- 1 red onion, peeled and finely diced
- 1 carrot, peeled and finely diced
- 1 celery stick, finely diced
- 1 leek, trimmed and chopped
- 1 red pepper, deseeded and chopped
- 100g (3½oz) chestnut mushrooms, finely chopped
- 2 garlic cloves, peeled and crushed
- 1 tbsp lemon juice
- 100g (3½oz) wholemeal breadcrumbs
- 1 tbsp chopped parsley
- 1 tbsp chopped oregano
- 75g (2½oz) mature Cheddar cheese, grated
- 1 egg, lightly beaten
- salt and pepper

Rich Tomato Sauce

- 2 red onion, peeled and finely diced
- 2 garlic clove, peeled and chopped
- 2 tbsp olive oil
- 2 x 400g tin chopped tomatoes
- 2 tsp balsamic vinegar
- 1 tsp brown sugar
- salt and pepper
- torn basil leaves

Gently fry the onions and garlic in olive oil until soft. Add the tomatoes and bring to the boil, before adding the balsamic vinegar, sugar and seasoning. Simmer on a low heat for 15–20 minutes, stirring occasionally. Check the seasoning, and serve with the torn basil leaves on top.

Sprouts Supreme

SERVES 8–10

450g (1lb) Brussels sprouts, trimmed
1 tbsp olive oil
2 garlic cloves, peeled and
  chopped
125ml (4fl oz) crème fraîche
freshly grated nutmeg
salt and pepper

With the slicing blade on a food processor, shred the sprouts thinly. Blanch them in boiling salted water for 2 minutes, then drain thoroughly. Gently heat the oil and garlic in a large saucepan, but do not let the garlic brown. Add the crème fraîche and sprouts and season. Turn into a serving dish and top liberally with the nutmeg.

Creamed Carrot and Mace

SERVES 8–10

900g (2lb) carrots, peeled and sliced
55g (2oz) butter, unsalted
1 tsp caster sugar
1 tsp grated orange zest
125ml (4fl oz) double cream
a sprinkling of powdered mace

Boil the carrots in salted water for 15–20 minutes, until soft. Drain and dry them thoroughly, and leave to cool. In a frying pan, melt the butter, add the sugar and orange zest. Whizz the cold carrots in a blender or pass them through a sieve until smooth. Add them to the buttery mixture and combine with the cream. Stir carefully until all of the purée is hot. Serve sprinkled with mace.

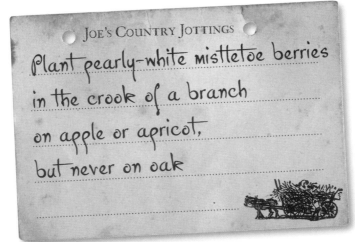

JOE'S COUNTRY JOTTINGS

Plant pearly-white mistletoe berries
in the crook of a branch
on apple or apricot,
but never on oak

Gran's Rich and Traditional Trifle

Christmas wouldn't have been Christmas without Gran's too-rich trifle. Grandad always puffed out his cheeks and let out his belt a notch or two when Gran proudly placed the cut glass bowl on her Christmas tea-table. I remember the gilded almonds nestling in the bed of cream always glinted in the flickering firelight.

SERVES 8–10

1 homemade sponge cake, or a packet of shop-bought Madeira cake
450g (1lb) jar apricot jam
250g (9oz) packet Amaretti biscuits
a generous glass of Amaretto
gilded almonds

For the custard:
300ml (½ pint) full cream milk
300ml (½ pint) double cream
8 egg yolks
1 tsp cornflour
25g (1oz) caster sugar
1 tbsp Amaretto

For the cream:
300ml (½ pint) double cream
1 tbsp Amaretto
1 tbsp icing sugar

First, make the custard. Beat the egg yolks with the cornflour and sugar until smooth. Bring the milk and cream to the boil and pour over the egg mixture, whisking continuously. Return to the pan and stir gently until the custard thickens. Cool slightly, and stir in the liqueur.

Split the sponge cakes, spread with jam and arrange in a glass serving bowl. Crumble the Amaretti biscuits onto the cake and splash with the liqueur. Pour over the custard and cool thoroughly, before chilling.

When ready to serve, whisk the double cream with the liqueur and icing sugar, and pile the cream onto the custard. Scatter with gilded almonds.

Caroline's Stirrup Cup

Served at the Boxing Day meet on Lord Netherbourne's estate – just when the foot was in the stirrup, hooves impatiently scuffing the gravel, pink jackets jostling, a mêlée of tail-wagging hounds. Then they were off – away and over the hill!

SERVES 20

3 bottles of full-bodied red wine
1 orange, stuck with 12 cloves
2 cinnamon sticks, halved
175g (6oz) caster sugar
½ tsp Angostura bitters
360ml (12fl oz) still spring water

Gently heat all the ingredients together in a large stainless steel saucepan, stirring to dissolve the sugar. Do not allow it to boil. Pour into a large punch bowl and serve in small glasses or mugs.

Roger's Oh-So-Sugary Shortbread

Roger Travers-Macy turned our lives upside down when he appeared unexpectedly for our daughter Debbie's 21st birthday. How could I have been so stupid and fallen for him all over again? He always was a smoothie.

MAKES ABOUT 15

115g (4oz) soft margarine
75g (3oz) caster sugar
½ beaten egg
a few drops of almond essence
150g (5oz) self-raising flour
40g (1½oz) desiccated coconut
a few glacé cherries, halved, to decorate

Preheat the oven to 160°C/325°F/Gas 3. Grease a baking tray. Beat together the margarine and sugar until creamy, then beat in the egg and almond essence. Add the flour and mix thoroughly. With wet hands, form the mixture into balls the size of a walnut and roll them in the coconut to coat. Place on the baking tray, leaving plenty of room for them to spread, and flatten each biscuit slightly with wet fingers. Decorate with pieces of glacé cherry. Bake for 20 minutes or until the biscuits are golden. Cool on the tray for 5 minutes before transferring to a wire rack to cool completely.

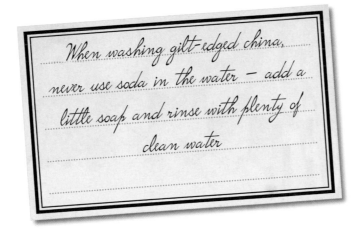

When washing gilt-edged china, never use soda in the water – add a little soap and rinse with plenty of clean water

JANUARY

1 TUE NEW YEAR'S DAY	**2** WED	**3** THU	**4** FRI	**5** SAT
8 TUE	**9** WED	**10** THU	**11** FRI	**12** SAT

PLOUGH MONDAY PUDDING

12oz self-raising flour
6oz chopped suet
¾ pint cold water
2 large onions, peeled and
    minced
½lb minced cold roast beef
½ tsp salt
½ tsp black pepper
½ pint pink beef gravy, to serve

Make the suet dough by mixing the flour and suet, adding the water drop-by-drop until a smooth dough. Roll out on a floured board. Mix the onion and meat, season and spread over the pastry. Wet the edges and roll in a muslin pudding cloth. Place in a pan of boiling water and boil gently for 2 hours. Serve with gravy.

Note: This can bubble away merrily on the range while Dan's out with Blossom and Boxer. Clean a mincer and remove all traces of meat and fat by passing a stale slice of bread through it.

15 TUE	**16** WED
19 SAT	**20** SUN
26 SAT	**27** SUN
29 TUE	**30** WED

6 SUN	7 MON *Jennifer's birthday*	**SAVOURY STUFFED ONIONS**

7 MON *Jennifer's birthday*

PLOUGH MONDAY

SAVOURY STUFFED ONIONS

4 onions
½lb sausagemeat
3oz butter
salt

Choose the onions as much the same size as possible. Peel them, then place in a saucepan large enough to hold them side-by-side and cover with cold water. Bring to the boil and simmer for 15 minutes. Take them out and drain well, standing them upside-down on a cloth. Scoop out the centres of the onions with a spoon, and fill the cavities with sausagemeat.

Melt the butter in a baking dish and stand the onions in it, side-by-side. Bake at 400ºF until nicely browned, basting occasionally with some of the butter. Stand the onions on a hot dish to serve.

6 SUN

13 SUN

14 MON

17 THU

18 FRI

21 MON

22 TUE

23 WED

24 THU

25 FRI

28 MON

31 THU

SWEET TREACLE SCONES

1lb flour
1½ tsp bicarbonate of soda
pinch of salt
1 tbsp sugar
1 tsp cream of tartar
1 tsp mixed spice
1oz butter
2 tbsp treacle
buttermilk

Sieve the dry ingredients into a basin and make a well in the centre. Heat the butter and treacle together and pour them into the well. Pour in gradually enough buttermilk to make a soft dough. Turn on to a floured board and knead lightly. Roll out to ½in thickness, cut into triangles and bake on a greased and floured tin for 15–20 minutes at 400ºF, until golden.

Chocolate Pye in Orange Crust

Jill always makes a special orange pastry for her Christmas mince pies, but sometimes she uses it with this rich chocolate filling instead. There were plates held out for seconds when she baked this tart for a Sunday lunch at Brookfield.

SERVES 6

2 tbsp lemon jelly marmalade
55g good-quality plain chocolate
115g (4oz) butter
75g (3oz) caster sugar
3 eggs, separated
75g (3oz) fine fresh breadcrumbs

For the orange pastry:
225g (8oz) plain flour
1 tbsp icing sugar
150g (5oz) unsalted butter, diced
1 egg yolk
grated zest of 1 orange
2 tbsp orange juice

To make the pastry, sift the flour and icing sugar into a bowl and rub in the butter until the mixture resembles breadcrumbs. Beat the egg yolk with the orange zest and juice. Make a well in the flour and pour in the egg yolk mixture, then stir together to make a dough, adding more orange juice if necessary. Wrap in cling film and chill for 30 minutes.

Preheat the oven to 190°C/375°F/Gas 5. Roll out the pastry and use to line a 23cm (9in) loose-bottomed flan tin. Cover with greaseproof paper, fill with baking beans and bake blind for 15–20 minutes, until pale golden. Remove from the oven, take out the paper and beans and leave to cool. Reduce the oven temperature to 180°C/350°F/Gas 4.

Gently heat the lemon jelly marmalade in a small pan with a tablespoon of water, stirring until smooth. Brush it over the base of the pastry case.

Melt the chocolate in a bowl set over a pan of hot water, making sure the water is not touching the base of the bowl. Remove from the heat. Cream the butter with the sugar until light and fluffy, then beat in the egg yolks and melted chocolate. Fold in the breadcrumbs. In a separate bowl, whisk the egg whites until they form soft peaks. Beat about a quarter of the whites into the chocolate mixture to loosen it and then fold in the rest with a metal spoon. Spoon the filling into the pastry case and spread it level. Bake for 25–30 minutes, until the filling springs back when pressed gently. Serve warm, with whipped or ice cream.

Jaxx Exquisite Chocolate Terrine with Crème Anglaise

Kenton tells me this has always been a firm favourite on the menu at Jaxx – much as Kenton believes he is with his female customers. I was grateful that he managed to tear himself away from the bar for long enough to scribble the recipe down.

SERVES 8–10

225g (8oz) good-quality plain chocolate
1 tbsp brandy
225g (8oz) unsalted butter, cut into pieces
200g (7oz) caster sugar
3 tbsp plain flour
1 tbsp cornflour
3 eggs

For the crème Anglaise:
1 egg plus 2 egg yolks
25g (1oz) caster sugar
1 vanilla pod
450ml (15fl oz) single cream

Preheat the oven to 160°C/325°F/Gas 3. Grease a 450g (1lb) loaf tin or terrine and line the base and sides with greaseproof paper, then grease the paper. Break up the chocolate and melt it with the brandy in a large bowl set over a pan of simmering water, making sure the water is not touching the base of the bowl. Add the butter and sugar, stirring until the butter has combined with the chocolate and the sugar has dissolved. Sift the flour and cornflour into the mixture and whisk for a few minutes while it heats through. Remove from the heat and then whisk in the eggs one by one.; the mixture will thicken and become slightly grainy but keep on whisking until it is smooth again. Pour into the prepared tin and place in a roasting tin half filled with water. Bake for about 45 minutes, until the mixture is firm and there is no movement when you shake the tin gently. Remove from the oven and leave to cool in the tin, then chill.

To make the crème Anglaise, put the egg, egg yolks and sugar in a bowl and beat well. Split open the vanilla pod and scrape out the seeds, then put the seeds and pod in a small heavy-based pan with the cream. Heat gently until the cream is almost boiling and then pour it on to the egg mixture, whisking constantly. Return the custard to the pan and cook over a low heat, stirring with a wooden spoon, until the mixture thickens enough to coat the back of the spoon. Do not let it get too hot or it will curdle. Remove from the heat and strain into a bowl, then cover and leave to cool, it will thicken more as it cools.

Serve the terrine in very thin slices, dusted with vanilla sugar or dredged with sugar mixed with cocoa powder, with a pool of crème Anglaise to complement it.

Debbie's Favourite
Rich Fruit Chocolate Cake

MAKES A 23CM (9IN) CAKE

225g (8oz) good-quality plain
chocolate, chopped
225g (8oz) unsalted butter
225g (8oz) light soft brown
sugar
4 eggs, beaten
250g (9oz) plain flour
25g (1oz) cocoa powder
1 tsp ground cinnamon
115g (4oz) walnuts, roughly
chopped
115g (4oz) almonds, roughly
chopped
115g (4oz) crystallised ginger,
115g (4oz) ready-to-eat
dried pineapple, chopped
115g (4oz) ready-to-eat
dried apricots, chopped
55g (2oz) candied peel, chopped
175g (6oz) raisins
grated zest of 1 orange

'To serve as a Christmas cake, cover with almond paste and ice as usual.'

Preheat the oven to 160°C/325°F/Gas 3. Grease and line a 23cm (9in) round cake tin. Break up the chocolate and melt it in a bowl set over a pan of hot water, making sure the water is not touching the base of the bowl.

Cream the butter and sugar together in a mixing bowl until light and fluffy, add the melted chocolate and beat until smooth. Add the beaten eggs, whisking well. Sift together the flour, cocoa and cinnamon and fold into the mixture. Fold in the nuts, ginger, pineapple, apricots, candied peel and raisins and grated orange zest. Turn the mixture into the prepared tin and level the surface. Bake for 1 hour, then reduce the oven temperature to 150°C/300°F/Gas 2 and bake for a further 1½–2 hours until a skewer inserted in the centre comes out clean. Leave to cool in the tin for 30 minutes, then turn out on a wire rack to cool completely.

To serve as a Christmas cake, cover with almond paste and ice as usual.

Debbie, my darling daughter, runs much of the farm in Hungary I'm sure with amazing skill, success and satisfaction. Oh if only I could see her happily married though.

The Bull's Best Sticky Toffee and Banana Pie

You need Jolene to organise one of her line dancing evenings to work this toothsome and delicious dessert off your hips. We don't all want to look that voluptuous, do we?

SERVES 6–8

150g (5oz) unsalted butter
175g (6oz) caster sugar
400g can condensed milk
2–3 ripe bananas
a little lemon juice
300ml (½ pint) double cream
1 tbsp (15ml) brandy
grated dark chocolate, to decorate

For the base:
225g (8oz) ginger biscuits
115g (4oz) unsalted butter

To make the base, put the biscuits in a plastic bag and crush to crumbs with a rolling pin, or crush them in a food processor. Melt the butter in a pan and stir in the crumbs. Press the mixture into a 20cm (8in) loose-bottomed flan tin and chill for 30 minutes.

Meanwhile, make the filling: melt the butter in a heavy-based pan, add the sugar and stir over a low heat until dissolved. Pour in the condensed milk and keep stirring until the mixture bubbles, thickens and turns caramel coloured. Pour over the biscuit base, leave to cool and then chill to set.

Slice the bananas and sprinkle with lemon juice to prevent discoloration, then arrange them on the caramel mixture. Whip the cream with the brandy and spread over the bananas. Decorate with grated chocolate and then chill again. Serve in small portions – it's disgracefully rich!

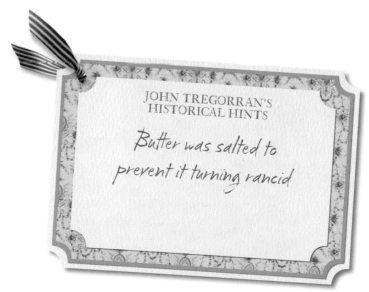

JOHN TREGORRAN'S
HISTORICAL HINTS

Butter was salted to prevent it turning rancid

Heather's Singin' Hinny

'Hey, Gran, that smells good' shrieks Ben as he and Josh race into the cosy Brookfield kitchen out of the cold yard. This reminds me of the time when my Gran, Doris Archer, was always floury-fingered and baking tea-time treats in that same kitchen many moons ago – for Tony, Lilian and me.

MAKES 10

225g (8oz) self-raising flour
½ tsp salt
½ tsp mixed spice
55g (2oz) butter
55g (2oz) lard
55g (2oz) currants
2–3 tbsp milk to mix

Sift the flour, salt and mixed spice together. Rub the butter and lard into it until it resembles fine breadcrumbs. Stir in the currants and mix in a little milk to make a thick paste. Roll out on a floured board and cut out 1.2cm (½in)-thick rounds with a scone cutter. Prick the tops and cook on a hot griddle, frying pan, or on a range hot plate. Cook for about 4 minutes on each side, until golden brown. Serve split open and buttered.

Point-to-Point Pheasant Pâté with Green Peppercorns

Prime place in the car park, alongside the paddock, tailgates are lowered and a picnic of dinner-party proportions has been prepared. Corks are popping and bubbles bubbling. Cheers to country life!

SERVES 6

225g (8oz) pork belly
225g (8oz) boned pheasant
225g (8oz) streaky bacon, zest removed
2 plump garlic cloves, peeled and crushed
1 tsp dried thyme or 1 tbsp chopped fresh thyme
½ tsp salt
1 tsp freshly ground black pepper
2 tsp green peppercorns in brine
2 tbsp red wine
4 tbsp brandy
8 smoked streaky bacon rashers

Chop the pork, pheasant and streaky bacon very finely or grind them in a food processor. Add the garlic, thyme, salt, pepper, green peppercorns, wine and brandy. Mix well, then cover and leave in a cool place to marinate for an hour or two.

Preheat the oven to 150°C/300°F/Gas 2. Line a 1 litre (2 pint) terrine with the rashers of smoked bacon, then pack the meat in tightly. Cover the terrine with a double layer of foil and place in a roasting tin half filled with water. Cook for 3 hours, then remove from the oven and leave to cool with a heavy weight on top of the pâté. When completely cold, chill overnight. Serve in slices, with sweet onion and thyme marmalade.

Sweet Onion and Thyme Marmalade

A perfect accompaniment to Point-to-Point Pheasant Pâté with Green Peppercorns (see opposite), venison sausages or, indeed, a haunch of venison. I'm always thinking of new ways to liven up my home-grown Home Farm venison and this is stunningly simple but very successful. 'Ten out of ten!' said Brian.

MAKES ABOUT 550G (1¼LB)

1 tbsp olive oil
15g (½oz) butter
450g (1lb) red onions, peeled and sliced
75g (3oz) soft brown sugar
1 tsp chopped thyme
225ml (7fl oz) red wine
4 tbsp raspberry or sherry vinegar
salt and pepper

Heat the olive oil and butter in a saucepan, stir in the onions, sugar and thyme and season with salt and pepper. Add the red wine and vinegar, cover and cook over a gentle heat for 30 minutes or until the liquid has evaporated and the onions are soft. Pour into a sterilised jar and seal while hot. Leave for 2 weeks to develop the flavour.

FEBRUARY

MARKET-DAY HOT POT

This can be left slowly cooking in a low oven while you go to market.

4 pork chops
2 pig's kidneys, sliced
2 large onions, peeled and sliced
2lb potatoes, peeled and sliced
1 tsp mixed herbs
1 tbsp brown sauce

Place all the ingredients in layers in a casserole dish. Season and pour over ½ pint of water. Cook slowly at 300ºF for 2–3 hours.

| **1** FRI GAME SHOOT ENDS |
| **3** SUN |
| **5** TUE |

11 MON	**12** TUE	**13** WED	**14** THU	**15** FRI
17 SUN	**18** MON	**19** TUE	**20** WED	**21** THU
23 SAT	**24** SUN	**25** MON	**26** TUE SHROVE TUESDAY	**27** WED

2

AT

ANDLEMAS

4

ON

MOTHER'S MOCK CRAB

½oz butter
1 large tomato, skinned and de-pipped
1 egg
1oz grated cheese
salt and pepper

Melt the butter and add the tomato. Simmer for 5 minutes. Beat the egg with the cheese and season well. Add to the tomato mixture and cook gently until thick. Use on hot toast, or cool for use as a sandwich filling.

5

WED

7

THU

8

FRI

9

SAT

10

SUN

6

AT

Little Tony's Birthday

22

RI

28

HU

SIMPLE SEVILLE ORANGE MARMALADE

Note: for each Seville orange allow ¾ pint of water, and ¾ lb of preserving sugar.

Halve the oranges and squeeze the juice into the water. Reserve the pips and any pith. Cut the orange peel first into quarters, and then cut into strips. Place the peel into the juice and water mix, and leave to stand overnight. Soak the pips and pith in a little water overnight, as well.

Strain the pips through a muslin cloth, and add the liquid to the peel, juice and water mix. Gently boil for 3 hours, until the peel is soft. Add the sugar and boil at a good rolling boil for another ¼ hour, or until it jellies. Tie down hot in clean glass jars.

SPRING

Springtime floods the floor of Leaders Wood, knee-deep in bluebells' shimmering haze, while buds burst and spray the hawthorn hedges green. Far off on Ten Elms Rise a cuckoo calls. In Manorfield Close, gleaming windows are flung open wide and fluffy blankets flap and wave on washing lines. Lynda's eager fingers pluck fresh spikes of aromatic herbs and clusters of the season's first new fruits to feature delicately in lunchtime's luxuries and supper's tempting treats.

Nora McAuley's Springtime Soda Bread

Nora, blonde, bold and resolute, worked as a barmaid at The Bull. Actually she had come across from Ireland to be with her precious Paddy, but things didn't work out. He left in a bit of a hurry, thank goodness! His legacy? Well, that's history now. Hers is this excellent soda bread, which Mum still bakes from time to time. If you can't get buttermilk, squeeze some lemon juice into ordinary milk and leave for 20 minutes to sour.

MAKES 2 SMALL LOAVES

225g (8oz) wholemeal flour
375g (13oz) strong plain flour
2 tsp salt
1 tsp bicarbonate of soda
25g (1oz) lard
1 spring onion, trimmed and finely chopped
2 tbsp chopped parsley
2 tbsp chopped tarragon
55g (2oz) medium oatmeal
600ml (1 pint) buttermilk or sour milk

Preheat the oven to 190°C/375°F/Gas 5. Grease a baking sheet. Sift the flours, salt and bicarbonate of soda into a bowl and rub in the lard. Stir in the spring onion, herbs and oatmeal, then mix to a loose dough with the milk, adding it a little at a time. Knead the dough lightly, just until smooth, and then shape into 2 loaves. Place on the baking sheet. Score the centre of each loaf with the back of a knife and sprinkle with a little wholemeal flour. Bake for about 30 minutes, until the loaves sound hollow when tapped underneath. Eat while fresh.

Lower Loxley's Creamy Leek, Apple and Celery Soup

Titcombe, proud to present his perfect pale green leeks, watches Hugh deftly and skillfully slice them into a creamy springtime soup.

SERVES 8

25g (1oz) butter
225g (8oz) celery, finely chopped
175g (6oz) potatoes, peeled and diced
4 leeks, trimmed and sliced, discarding those dark green tops
175g (6oz) apple, peeled, cored and chopped
600ml (1 pint) chicken or turkey stock (or bouillon)
115g (4oz) crème fraîche
150ml (5fl oz) milk
salt and pepper
a handful of pale celery leaves

In a large pan, melt the butter over a gentle heat. Stir in the celery, potatoes, leeks and apples. Cover and cook gently for 5 minutes. Add the stock, cover and simmer gently for 20–25 minutes, until the vegetables are tender. Purée in a blender until smooth, stir in the crème fraîche and milk, and season to taste.

Re-heat before serving scattered with the chopped celery leaves. This soup is delicious served with Lower Loxley's Cheese and Lovage Country Loaf.

Cheese and Lovage Country Loaf

Served by chef Hugh, with a bowlful of 'soup of the day' in the Orangery.

MAKES 1 SMALL LOAF

225g (8oz) self-raising flour
1 tsp bicarbonate of soda
½ tsp salt
115g (4oz) wholemeal flour

25–55g (1–2oz) lard or block margarine
75g (3oz) Cheddar cheese, grated
2 large leaves of lovage, finely snipped
1 spring onion, trimmed and finely chopped
450ml (¾ pint) buttermilk
(or milk with a dash of lemon juice)

Preheat the oven to 190°C/375°F/Gas 5. Grease a baking tray. Sift the dry ingredients together, then rub in the lard. Stir in 55g (2oz) of the cheese, then the lovage and onion, and mix to a soft dough with the milk, adding a little at a time. Knead the dough lightly and then shape into a 17cm (7in) round and mark into triangles. Sprinkle with the remaining cheese, place on the tray and bake for 45 minutes.

Nelson's Criss-Cross Salmon Tart

Escaping through an archway from Borchester's melée into the market town's haven, Nelson's Café Bar dispensed hospitality with stylish charm and a certain elegance. It was a shopper's haven.

Serve the tart warm, with a sauce of fromage frais whipped together with lemon juice, chopped dill and parsley.

SERVES 6

25g (1oz) fresh breadcrumbs
4 tbsp milk, plus extra for brushing
25g (1oz) butter
½ an onion, peeled and finely chopped
2 hard-boiled eggs, chopped
350g (12oz) cooked salmon, boned and flaked
4 tbsp extra virgin olive oil
1 tbsp lemon juice
2 tsp finely chopped dill
2 tbsp finely chopped parsley
salt and pepper

For the pastry:
225g (8oz) plain flour
pinch of salt
115g (4oz) chilled butter
115g (4oz) Cheddar cheese, finely grated
a little iced water, to bind

To make the pastry, sift the flour and salt into a bowl, then grate in the butter and rub it in with your fingertips. Stir in the grated cheese and enough iced water to make a firm dough. Wrap in cling film and chill for 30 minutes. Preheat the oven to 200°C/400°F/Gas 6.

Meanwhile, put the breadcrumbs to soak in the milk. Melt the butter in a small pan and gently cook the onion until soft, then remove from the heat. Mix the onion and butter with the hard-boiled eggs, fish, soaked breadcrumbs, olive oil, lemon juice and herbs. Season to taste.

Roll out about two-thirds of the pastry and use to line a 23cm (9in) flan tin. Spoon the filling into the pastry case and spread level. Roll out the remaining pastry and cut it into long, thin strips. Use these to make a lattice over the pie, pressing the edges together well to seal. Brush the pastry with milk and bake for 15 minutes, then reduce the oven temperature to 180°C/350°F/Gas 4 and bake for a further 15–20 minutes, until the pastry is a deep golden colour.

MARCH

SPICY EASTER BISCUITS

5oz margarine
5oz caster sugar
1 egg, beaten
2oz currants
8oz plain flour
1 tsp ground cinnamon

Cream the margarine and the sugar until light and fluffy, then slowly add the beaten egg, mixing well. Add the currants, and then gradually sift in the flour and cinnamon. Roll out and cut into rounds with a biscuit cutter. Bake at 450ºF until golden.

1 SAT	2 SUN
6 THU	7 FRI
11 TUE	12 WED	13 THU

17 MON	18 TUE
24 MON	25 TUE
	LADY DAY
28 FRI	29 SAT

PLAIN RICE PUDDING

3oz rice
1½ pint of milk
2oz butter
2oz sugar
2 eggs, well-whisked
grated zest of 1 lemon

Wash the rice, and about half cook it in boiling water. Drain off the water and put the rice into a stewpan with the milk. Stew slowly until the rice is quite tender, and just before it is taken from the fire, stir in the butter and sugar. Remove it from the fire, and when it has cooled a little add the eggs and the grated lemon zest. Pour into a well-buttered pie dish and bake at 250ºF for 30–40 minutes.

Note: nutmeg can be used instead of the lemon.

3 MON	**4** TUE	**5** WED	
8 SAT	**9** SUN	**10** MON	
14 FRI	**15** SAT	**16** SUN	
19 WED	**20** THU	**21** FRI	**22** SAT	**23** SUN MOTHERING SUNDAY
26 WED	**27** THU		
30 SUN	**31** MON		

QUICK POTTED MEAT

1lb beef steak
2 tbsp water
2 cloves
4 peppercorns
a grating of nutmeg
1 tsp salt
½ tsp pepper
½ tsp cayenne pepper
1oz butter

Stew the beef with the water, cloves and peppercorns until tender. Put through a mincer twice. Add the salt, the rest of the spices and butter. Put into pots and seal with melted butter.

STUFFED SPRING LAMB

1 shoulder of lamb
3oz fine breadcrumbs
2 tbsp shredded suet
4 tsp chopped parsley and mint
salt and pepper
1 egg, beaten with a little milk

Remove the meat from the lamb in one piece. Mix the stuffing ingredients together and spread on the meat. Roll up carefully and secure with meat skewers. Dust with flour, season well and roast at 350ºF for 1½ hours.

Susan's Simple Salmon and Parsley Fishcakes

Susan says she always keeps a pot of parsley on the kitchen window ledge 'then I can snip fresh green leaves onto my savouries all year round. The anchovy essence was ordered by Sabrina Thwaite, so thought I'd give it a try.'

MAKES 4 FISHCAKES

225g (8oz) potatoes, peeled and quartered (Desirée are excellent)
225g (8oz) salmon tail, or a small tin will do
½ tsp anchovy essence
1 heaped tbsp chopped parsley
salt and pepper
2 tbsp plain flour, seasoned
1 egg, beaten
4 tbsp fresh white breadcrumbs
vegetable oil for frying

Boil and mash the potatoes with a nut of butter and splash of milk. Poach the salmon in water for 5 minutes (if using fresh). Drain and flake it into the potato, adding the anchovy essence. Add the chopped parsley and season. Allow to cool.

Using your hands (wash them first!), shape the mixture into cakes. Dip each into the flour, then the beaten egg before coating thoroughly in breadcrumbs. Fry gently in shallow oil until golden brown. Serve with a wedge of lemon and a scattering of parsley.

JOE'S COUNTRY JOTTINGS

*If many fogs in March you see
Then many frosts in May will be*

Caroline's Crunchy Crabcakes

There's always been something especially smooth and sophisticated about Caroline. Maybe that's what Brian saw in her all those years ago. So it's not just simple, plain fishcakes, oh no! It's sophisticated crabcakes with a smooth celeriac cream.

MAKES 6 CRABCAKES

150g (5oz) potatoes, peeled and chopped
   into chunks
150g (5oz) sweet potatoes, peeled
   and chopped into chunks
300g (10oz) cooked crabmeat, diced
   or crumbled
1 handful fresh parsley, chopped
squeeze of lemon juice
salt and pepper
corn oil for frying

Boil the potatoes and sweet potatoes and drain thoroughly. Mash and combine with the crabmeat, parsley and lemon juice. Season well, and allow to cool completely. Form into smallish balls about 2.5cm (1in) in diameter (the mix should make about 12), and fry in hot oil, turning often, until brown and crispy.

   Serve with wedges of lemon and lime.

Smooth Celeriac Cream

SERVES 6–8

1 large root celeriac
juice of 1 large lemon
small tub of crème fraîche
salt and pepper

Peel the celeriac and rinse. Chop into large chunks and sprinkle with lemon juice. Cook in salted water for about 30 minutes until tender. Drain and allow to dry in the saucepan. Pass through a vegetable sieve or whizz in a blender. Fold in the crème fraîche and season to taste.

Betty's Thrifty Tart

Pennies were in short supply at Willow Farm, especially after Mike's accident, so 'waste not, want not' was Betty's motto – a wise saying for us all to remember.

SERVES 4

55g (2oz) onion, peeled and
  finely chopped
25g (1oz) butter or margarine
55g (2oz) Cheddar cheese, grated
2 eggs, lightly beaten
300ml (½ pint) milk
1 tsp each chopped parsley, chives,
  lovage and tarragon
salt and pepper

For the pastry:
225g (8oz) plain or wholemeal flour
pinch of salt
225g (8oz) margarine, diced
55g (2oz) lard, diced
a little iced water, to bind

To make the pastry, sift the flour and salt into a bowl and then rub in the margarine and lard until the mixture resembles breadcrumbs. Add 3–4 tbsp iced water and mix to a pliable dough.

Wrap in cling film and chill for 30 minutes.

Preheat the oven to 200°C/400°F/Gas 6. Roll out the pastry and use to line a 20cm (8in) flan tin or pie plate. Cook the onion in the butter or margarine until soft and translucent, then place in the pastry case. Mix together the cheese, eggs, milk and herbs and season with salt and pepper. Pour the mixture into the pastry case and bake for 35 minutes or until the filling is set and the pastry golden.

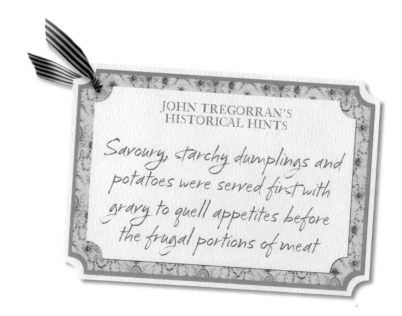

JOHN TREGORRAN'S
HISTORICAL HINTS

Savoury, starchy dumplings and potatoes were served first with gravy to quell appetites before the frugal portions of meat

Hassett Hill's Spring Casserole

It's one thing seeing their little woolly bodies gamboling on the distant hills — it's another thing enjoying the delicious, delicate flavour of lamb at the dinner table. 'But hey-ho, that's farming for you,' chuckled Brian, mopping a drip of gravy from his stripy silk tie.

SERVES 4

1 tbsp olive oil
4 lamb neck fillets, cubed
2 garlic cloves, peeled and crushed
200g (7oz) baby carrots, cut into pieces
200g (7oz) courgettes, cut into 1cm (½in) rings
4 sun-dried tomatoes, finely chopped
1 tbsp plain flour
500ml (1 pint) chicken stock (or bouillon)
1 sprig of rosemary
salt and pepper
2 tbsp chopped mint

Preheat the oven to 150°C/300°F/ Gas 2. Heat the oil in a large casserole. Brown the lamb in batches and remove onto kitchen paper to drain. Soften the garlic in the oil, before adding the carrots, courgettes and tomatoes and sauté gently. Return the lamb to the casserole, stir in the flour and gradually add the stock. Add the rosemary sprig and season with salt and pepper and bring to the boil, skimming off any foam. Cook in the oven for 40 minutes.

Sprinkle with the chopped mint just before serving, and eat with Tony's early new potatoes.

Dear son-in-law Ian suggested this oh-so-easy recipe to me so that I could impress Brian's last-minute Borchester Land guests with an almost impromptu supper.

QuickSuppers

Lemon, Ginger and Honey-glazed Duck

SERVES 4

4 duck breast fillets
(about 250g/9oz each)
salt and pepper
125ml (4fl oz) of water
55g (2oz) stem ginger, chopped
2 tbsp runny honey
juice from half a large lemon

Preheat the oven to 200ºC/400ºF/Gas 6. Score the fat on the duck skin and season. Heat a stove-top grill pan until hot. Add the duck breasts, skin-side down, and sear for a couple of minutes until the skin is crispy. Transfer to a roasting tin with the juices. Cook in the oven for 20–25 minutes. Remove from the oven and keep warm under foil until required.

For the sauce, dissolve the sugar in water and boil for 3–4 minutes. Add the ginger, honey and lemon juice, and stir until thick and syrupy. Serve the duck with the glaze poured over the top.

 Preparation time **5 mins**
Cooking time **35 mins**

Côtes de Veau à la Bonne Ferme

Voluble Vicky Tucker over at Willow Farm went into veal production. Oh well, you have to admire her tenacity – what a pity she wasn't successful. Personally, I prefer to use pork anyway.

SERVES 4

4 tbsp olive oil
4 veal chops, trimmed of excess fat
1 head of chicory, sliced
6 small new potatoes, peeled and thinly sliced
6 small onions, peeled and sliced
1 garlic clove, peeled and crushed
4 rashers of smoked bacon, chopped
grated zest and juice of 1 orange
1 tsp sugar
salt and pepper
250ml (8fl oz) white wine

Preheat the oven to 180°C/350°F/Gas 4. Heat 2 tbsp of oil in a flameproof casserole and sauté the chops over a low heat until browned. Add the chicory, fry for a couple of minutes and then remove both the meat and chicory to a plate and keep warm.

Heat the remaining oil and sauté the potatoes, onions, garlic and bacon for 2–3 minutes. Add the zest and juice of the orange and the sugar. Season well, then add the wine. Bring the sauce to the boil and simmer for 3–4 minutes. Return the chops and braised chicory to the casserole, cover and cook in the oven at for 1 hour. Serve with a crisp green salad.

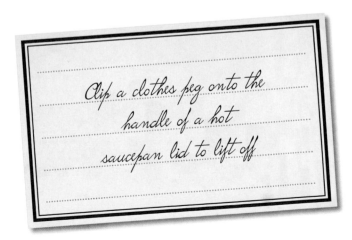

Clip a clothes peg onto the handle of a hot saucepan lid to lift off

APRIL

CIDER-BAKED HAM

4½–5lb ham joint
2 onions, peeled
3 carrots, peeled
3 celery sticks
12 cloves
½ pint cider
demerara sugar

Soak the ham in cold water overnight. Drain and put into a pan with enough water to cover. Roughly cut the vegetables into pieces and add to the pan. Simmer gently, allowing 25 minutes per lb of meat, but subtracting 40 minutes from the total. At the end of the time, remove the pan from the heat and leave for 30 minutes.

Lift the ham from the liquid, place in a baking tin, remove the skin and stud the fat with the cloves. Pour over the cider, and then spread thickly with the sugar. Bake at 350ºF for 40 minutes, basting three times with the cider during this period. Lift on to a rack to cool. Stand the rack on a dish and baste a further 2–3 times as it cools.

1 TUE	**2** WED
6 SUN	**7** MON
11 FRI	**12** SAT
16 WED	**17** THU

18 FRI	**19** SAT	**20** SUN	**21** MON	**22** TUE
25 FRI	**26** SAT	**27** SUN	**28** MON	**29** TUE

3	4	5
THU	**FRI**	**SAT**

8	9	10
TUE	**WED**	**THU**

13	14	15
SUN	**MON**	**TUE**

PROUD QUEEN'S PUDDING

1 cup white breadcrumbs
grated zest of 1 lemon
½ pint milk
1oz butter
2 tsp demerara sugar
2 eggs, separated
2 tbsp marmalade
4oz caster sugar

Mix the breadcrumbs with the lemon zest. Heat the milk, butter and sugar and pour over the breadcrumbs and lemon zest. Beat and add the egg yolks, stirring them in carefully. Pour into a buttered pie dish and bake for 1 hour at 300ºF.

Remove from the oven and spread the top with marmalade. Whip the whites of the eggs with the caster sugar until stiff, then spread on the pudding. Return to the oven and bake until the meringue is set.

23	24
WED	**THU**
Phil's birthday	

30	
WED	

SPRING RHUBARB CHUTNEY

2lb rhubarb
zest and juice of 2 lemons
zest and juice of 1 orange
1oz garlic, finely chopped
1 pint/16fl oz vinegar
1lb sultanas
1oz salt
½ tsp white pepper
2lb brown sugar
1oz fresh ginger root, bruised

Skin the rhubarb and cut into 1in pieces. Peel the lemons and orange thinly. Put all the ingredients, except the sugar and ginger, through a mincer. Place in a large stewpan, with the sugar and whole ginger root, and simmer on a low heat, stirring frequently. When soft and a thick pulp remove the ginger. Place in clean jars and cover. This chutney improves with keeping.

Kate's Falafel

It's hard to remember Kate and Roy travelling the countryside in a clapped-out van. But they did, and they sold their spicy ethnic foods at funny muddy festivals and folksy gatherings.

MAKES 10

450g (1lb) dried chickpeas
1 large onion, peeled and chopped
3 garlic cloves, peeled and chopped
4 spring onions, trimmed and chopped
1 tsp baking powder
1 tsp ground cumin
large bunch of coriander, chopped
large bunch of flat-leafed parsley, chopped
1 tbsp buckwheat flour
vegetable oil for deep-frying

Soak the chickpeas in water overnight, then drain. Cover with fresh water, bring to the boil and simmer until tender, then drain very thoroughly (or you could use tinned chickpeas, which don't need soaking). Put all the ingredients except the oil in a food processor. Process until the paste is smooth but not completely puréed. Take small lumps of the mixture in your hands and form into patties 5cm (2in) in diameter and 2cm (¾in) thick. Deep-fry them in hot oil, turning if necessary, until golden on both sides, then drain on kitchen paper. Serve with pitta bread, Kate's Simple Hummus (opposite) and salad. The falafel can be made in advance and reheated in the oven if necessary.

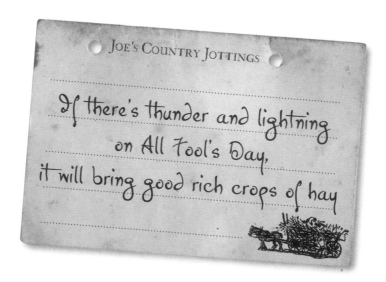

JOE'S COUNTRY JOTTINGS

If there's thunder and lightning on All Fool's Day, it will bring good rich crops of hay

Kate's Simple Hummus

'It's healthy, wholesome, rich in calcium and protein', Kate tells us, 'and great served as a sauce with grilled vegetables or as a dip with pitta bread.'

SERVES 8

225g (8oz) dried chickpeas
4 garlic cloves, peeled and crushed
juice of 3 lemons
2 tbsp olive oil
150ml (5fl oz) tahini paste
½ tsp ground cumin
½ tsp ground coriander
2 tbsp chopped coriander leaves
salt and pepper

Soak the chickpeas in water to cover overnight, then drain. Cover with fresh water, bring to the boil and simmer until tender, then drain again, reserving the liquid. Place the chickpeas in a food processor with the garlic, lemon juice, olive oil, tahini paste, ground spices and a little of the reserved cooking liquid. Purée to a thick paste, adding more cooking liquid if necessary. Fold in most of the chopped coriander leaves and season to taste with salt and pepper. Serve in a shallow bowl, garnished with the remaining coriander.

Avocado Chilli Dip

Perfect for rolling up in a wrap with shredded lettuce, cooked chicken and a dollop of cream cheese. Pop it into pitta pockets, too, but don't forget to put the avocado stone in the dip to stop it discolouring.

SERVES 4–6

2 ripe avocados
1 large tomato, skinned, deseeded
    and finely chopped
1 fresh chilli, deseeded and
    finely chopped
1 small onion, peeled and finely
    chopped
1 tbsp lemon juice
½ tsp Tabasco sauce
1 tbsp chopped coriander
salt and pepper

Peel, stone and mash the avocados. Combine with all the remaining ingredients, adjusting the seasoning to taste. Cover the dish with cling film and leave for an hour or so before serving, to enhance the flavour.

Lynda's Dab, Dill and Scallop Pie

After patiently explaining to me that dabs, didn't I know, are just small, young plaice, Lynda then proudly pointed to the delicate fronds of dill feathering the herb beds at Ambridge Hall.

SERVES 8

1.1kg (2½lb) floury potatoes, peeled
6 whole dabs, skinned (or 8 plaice fillets)
125ml (4fl oz) dry white wine
12 scallops, shelled and cleaned
2 shallots, peeled and finely chopped
55g (2oz) butter
250ml (½ pint) single cream or crème fraîche
1 tsp finely chopped dill
salt and pepper
2 tsp chopped parsley

Preheat the oven to 190°C/375°F/Gas 5. Boil and mash the potatoes well with a little butter and cream. Poach the skinned fish for 5–10 minutes (depending on size) in water or milk, then remove and drain. Sauté the shallots in the butter until soft, then pour on the wine and simmer until reduced by half. Add the cream or crème fraîche, and the dill. Place the fish and cream sauce in a large, ovenproof dish. Spread the mashed potato on top, and dot with butter. Bake for 25–30 minutes until golden.

Sprinkle with the chopped parsley just before serving.

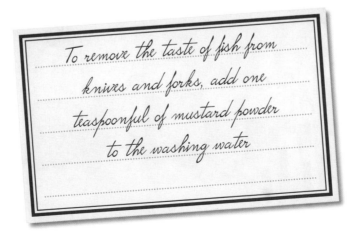

To remove the taste of fish from knives and forks, add one teaspoonful of mustard powder to the washing water

My Mediterranean Fish Stew

Blithely imagining that Brian and I would retire to a hill-top hideaway, wild thyme scenting the air while the azure sea shimmered in the distance, I thought I would turn my culinary skills to a tempting Mediterranean dish. It was simple to create but not so simple to tempt my husband away from Ambridge.

SERVES 6

2 tbsp olive oil

1 red onion, peeled and chopped

2 cloves of garlic, peeled and chopped

1 large red pepper, cored, deseeded and
   cut into ribbons

100ml (3½fl oz) dry white wine

400g tin of chopped tomatoes

2 potatoes, peeled and cut into chunks

700g (1½lb) fish, such as cod, salmon,
   hake and coley

12 prawns

salt and pepper

2 tsp capers, chopped

handful flat-leaf parsley, chopped

Heat the oil in a large pan, stir in the onions, garlic and red pepper and fry until soft. Add the wine, tomatoes and potatoes and cook gently for 15–20 minutes, until the potatoes are just tender. Add the fish and prawns, and cook slowly for 10 minutes. Season, scatter over the capers and parsley, and serve.

This is delicious served with chunks of crusty bread and, depending on the weather, a crisp green salad.

Spring Herb and Goat's Cheese Tart

Lynda's god-like goats, Demeter and Persephone, used to nibble greedily at the greener-than-green grass at Ambridge Hall.

SERVES 6

3 spring onions, trimmed and finely
    chopped
1 tbsp extra virgin olive oil
175ml (6fl oz) crème fraîche
1 tsp Dijon mustard
1 garlic clove, peeled and crushed
a handful of chopped mixed parsley,
    chervil, tarragon and lovage
3 eggs, beaten
175g (6oz) goat's cheese, rind removed
salt and pepper

For the pastry:
225g (8oz) plain flour
pinch of salt
115g (4oz) butter, diced
1 egg yolk
a little iced water to bind

To make the pastry, sift the flour and salt into a bowl and rub in the butter, then add the egg yolk and enough iced water to make a reasonably firm dough. Wrap in cling film and chill for 30 minutes. Preheat the oven to 200°C/400°F/Gas 6.

Roll out the pastry and use to line a 23cm (9in) loose-bottomed flan tin. Cover with greaseproof paper, fill with baking beans and bake blind for 15–20 minutes. Remove from the oven, take out the paper and beans and leave to cool.

Meanwhile, sweat the spring onions gently in the olive oil in a heavy-based pan until they are soft but not browned. Add the crème fraîche and mustard and bring to the boil, then add the garlic, herbs and some salt and pepper to taste. Cool this mixture slightly, then add it to the beaten eggs and mix together thoroughly.

Crumble the goat's cheese into the pastry shell and pour the cream mixture over the top. Bake for 20–25 minutes, until puffed up and golden brown.

Smoked Trout & Asparagus Terrine

6 asparagus spears
450g (1lb) smoked trout
115g (4oz) fromage frais
90ml (3fl oz) sunflower oil
3 eggs
grated zest and juice of 1 lemon
115g (4oz) smoked salmon
cut into strips
lemon and lime wedges and
sprigs of parsley, to garnish

Preheat the oven to 160°C/325°F/ Gas 3. Trim the asparagus spears and cook them in lightly salted boiling water for 2–3 minutes until just tender, then drain. Remove any skin and bones from the trout and place it in a food processor with the fromage frais, oil, eggs, and lemon zest and juice. Blend well.

Grease a 900g (2lb) loaf tin or terrine and tip one-third of the mixture into it. Arrange the asparagus spears on top. Cover with half the remaining mixture and place the smoked salmon strips on top of that. Finally, cover with the remaining trout mixture. Cover the tin with greaseproof paper and foil and place in a roasting tin half filled with water. Bake for 1 hour. Leave to cool in the tin and then chill. Turn out on to a serving plate and garnish with lemon and lime wedges and parsley.

'Trim the asparagus spears and cook them in lightly salted boiling water...'

This is a delectable supper dish with a pound of Underwoods' fine smoked trout and a few fat spears of Jill's asparagus.

MAY

RABBIT RAGOUT

1 rabbit
seasoned flour
12oz onions, peeled
3 leeks
4 celery sticks
4oz streaky bacon
dripping
stock
seasoning

For the dumplings:
3½o½z flour
2oz shredded suet
½ onion, peeled and
  chopped
salt and pepper
cold water to mix

Joint the rabbit and soak in salt and water. Dry joints and toss in the seasoned flour. Place in a fire-proof dish. Slice the onions, chop the leeks and celery and add to the dish. Dice the bacon rashers and add. Dot with dripping.

Add the stock to halfway up the dish, season and cook in the oven for one hour at 300ºF. Meanwhile, make the dumplings by mixing the flour, suet, onions and seasoning together, and add enough water to bind. Roll into balls.

Remove the rabbit from the oven, stir and add the dumplings. Return to the oven for a further half hour.

1 THU *Morris dancing on village green* MAY DAY	**2** FRI
6 TUE	**7** WED
11 SUN	**12** MON
18 SUN	**19** MON
22 THU	**23** FRI

26 MON	**27** TUE	**28** WED	**29** THU OAK APPLE DAY	**30** FRI

3 AT	**MAY DAY SALAD** Rinse and thoroughly dry a cabbage lettuce. Grate some carrot, turnip and fresh radishes. Dice some cooked beetroot and finely chop a bunch of spring onions. Pile some lettuce on plates and arrange a spoonful of each vegetable around. Pour on some salad cream or mayonnaise. Serve immediately.	**4** SUN	**5** MON
8 HU		**9** FRI	**10** SAT
13 UE	**14** WED	**15** THU	**16** FRI	**17** SAT
20 UE	**21** WED		**MAY-TIME MELTING MOMENTS** 3oz butter or margarine 1½oz caster sugar 1 egg, beaten 4oz cornflour ½ tbsp baking powder drop of lemon essence Beat together the butter and sugar. Stir in the egg, cornflour and baking powder and lemon essence. Mix to a thick cream. Bake in bun cases for 10–15 minutes in a moderate oven.
24 SAT	**25** SUN		
31 SAT			

sparrowgrass and Scallion Frittata

Dear old Bert would never allow this recipe to be called an asparagus and spring onion frittata. 'Asparagus, my eye, that's not what it's called – it's sparrowgrass and allus has bin – and these, them's scallions.' And who am I to argue?

SERVES 8

225g (8oz) waxy new potatoes, scrubbed
225g (8oz) asparagus
1 bunch of spring onions or scallions
6 eggs
salt and pepper
55g (2oz) Parmesan cheese, freshly grated
55g (2oz) butter
4 tbsp parsley, chopped

Boil the potatoes until nearly soft, then cool and slice. Rinse and trim the asparagus, snapping off the woody bottoms of the stems. Boil until just tender (2–3 minutes), then drain.

Trim the spring onions and slice thinly. Beat the eggs thoroughly and add seasoning and half the Parmesan cheese, then stir in the asparagus, potatoes and spring onions.

Melt the butter in a large cast iron frying pan 25cm (10in) in diameter, and pour in the egg mixture. Cook for about 8 minutes over a low heat, until the frittata is beginning to set. Remove the pan from the heat and place under a low grill until the frittata is completely set and turning golden brown.

To serve, sprinkle on the rest of the Parmesan and the chopped parsley, and cut into wedges. This is delicious served hot or cold.

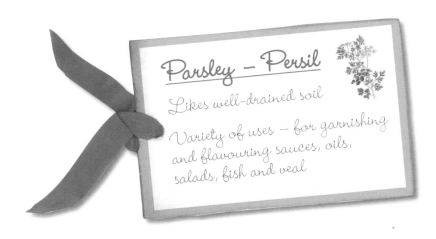

Parsley – Persil

Likes well-drained soil

Variety of uses – for garnishing and flavouring sauces, oils, salads, fish and veal

Julia's Potato and Red Pepper Omelette

The late rather grand Julia Pargetter learned to make this simple supper dish when visiting sister Ellen in sunny Spain. Tapas, tortillas, tarantellas and a chilled glass of sangria...aah. Hasta la vista!

SERVES 6

2 large potatoes, peeled and diced
olive oil for frying
1 small red onion, peeled and chopped
1 red pepper, peeled, deseeded and chopped
8 eggs, lightly beaten
salt and pepper

Blanch the diced potatoes in boiling water for 2 minutes, then drain well and pat dry on kitchen paper. Heat a few tablespoons of olive oil in a heavy-based 25cm (10in) frying pan. Sauté the onion and red pepper until they are beginning to soften but not brown. Add the potatoes to the beaten eggs, mix thoroughly and season well. Pour this into the frying pan and stir to mix with the onion and pepper. Cover and cook over a very low heat for 15–20 minutes, until the eggs are beginning to set. Run a knife around the edge and shake the pan to prevent the omelette sticking, then turn the omelette over with a spatula or turn it on to a large plate. Add some more oil to the pan and cook the omelette on the reverse side until golden underneath. Serve hot or at room temperature, cut into wedges.

Shula's Citrus Crème Brulée

It was Ed Grundy's beautiful Guernseys that gave Shula the idea of buying thick yellow Channel Island cream for her favourite crème brulée. She says the citrus flavour cuts across the undoubted richness.

SERVES 6

600ml (1 pint) Channel Island double cream
finely grated zest of 1 orange and 1 lemon
1 cinnamon stick
4 egg yolks
115g (4oz) caster sugar

Preheat the oven to 150°C/300°F/Gas 2. Pour the cream into a bowl set over a pan of simmering water, making sure the water is not touching the base of the bowl. Heat gently, then add the orange and lemon zest and cinnamon stick and leave to infuse for 15 minutes over a low heat. Remove the cinnamon stick.

Beat the egg yolks and 55g (2oz) of the sugar together until light in colour. Gradually pour on the cream, stirring with a whisk until smooth. Pour the custard into 6 ramekin dishes or a shallow baking dish. Stand in a roasting tin containing enough hot water to reach halfway up the sides of the dishes. Bake for about 1 hour, until just set, then remove from the oven and leave to cool. Chill overnight.

Before serving, sprinkle the remaining sugar over the top of the custard and put under a very hot grill for 2–3 minutes (or use a blowtorch) to caramelise the sugar.

Mary-Jo's Banana Bread

On their return from the American trip, Robert and Lynda discovered a loaf of Mary-Jo's homemade banana bread on the pantry shelf at Ambridge Hall with a little note: 'To remember U.S. by!'

MAKES A 900G (2LB) LOAF

115g (4oz) butter
115g (4oz) soft brown sugar
2 eggs, beaten
½ tsp vanilla essence
250g (9oz) plain flour
2 tsp baking powder
½ tsp salt
3 ripe bananas, mashed
75g (3oz) pecan nuts, chopped

Preheat the oven to 180°C/350°F/Gas 4. Grease and line the base of a 900g (2lb) loaf tin. Cream the butter with the sugar until soft and pale, then beat in the eggs and vanilla essence. Sift the dry ingredients together and fold into the creamed mixture alternately with the mashed bananas. Fold in the nuts. Turn into the prepared tin and bake for about an hour, until well-risen and golden brown. Cool in the tin for 10 minutes before turning out on a wire rack to cool completely.

JOHN TREGORRAN'S
HISTORICAL HINTS

Eggs and cream used to be whisked with twigs or feathers

Nigel's Nanny's Nursery Pudding

The lovable Nigel Pargetter was cared for in those innocent formative years by a doting nanny. If Nigel was good, it was syrupy pud – and even a spoonful for his precious teddy bear, Tiddles.

SERVES 6

115g (4oz) **unsalted butter**
115g (4oz) **caster sugar**
grated zest and juice of 1 orange
2 eggs, beaten
175g (6oz) **self-raising flour, sifted**
90ml (3fl oz) **golden syrup**

Preheat the oven to 160°C/325°F/Gas 3. Grease a 1.2 litre (2 pint) pudding basin. In a mixing bowl cream the butter and sugar together until pale and fluffy. Beat in the orange zest and juice, and then beat in the eggs, a little at a time. Fold in the flour.

Spoon the syrup into a greased the pudding basin and then spoon in the sponge mixture. Cover the basin with pleated greaseproof paper or foil and place in a roasting tin three-quarters filled with water. Bake for 1½ hours, until risen and firm, topping up the water in the roasting tin if necessary. Turn out and serve with a jug of warmed golden syrup mixed with fresh orange juice.

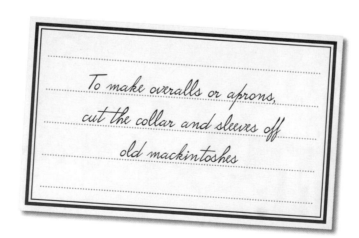

To make overalls or aprons, cut the collar and sleeves off old mackintoshes

Laurence Lovell's Lemon Crunch

I imagine nothing could have made Laurence happier than lolling back on his sofa listening to a sweet melody of Ivor Novello's, sipping a sweet sherry and nibbling a sugary lemon crunch. Oh dear, perhaps I'm being unkind!

MAKES ABOUT 16

115g (4oz) unsalted butter
115g (4oz) caster sugar, plus extra for coating
1 egg, beaten
grated zest of 1½ lemons
225g (8oz) self-raising flour, sifted

Preheat the oven to 180°C/350°F/Gas 4. Grease a baking tray. Cream the butter and sugar together until soft and pale. Beat in the egg, followed by the lemon zest, and then fold in the flour. Flour your hands lightly and form the mixture into little round cushions the size of a walnut. Roll them in caster sugar to coat. Place them on the baking tray, flattening each cushion slightly with the palm of your hand. Bake for 15–20 minutes, until pale golden. Cool on the baking tray for 5 minutes before transferring them to a wire rack to cool completely.

Grey Gables Coffee Granita and Brandy Syllabub

Grey Gables Hotel, owned now by Caroline and Oliver Sterling, is set within acres of green and glorious parkland. It offers elegant facilities and exquisite cuisine in the bistro and full restaurant, excellently prepared by Adam's partner, Ian.

SERVES 6–8

For the coffee granita:
750ml (1¼ pints) water
6 tbsp instant coffee granules
150g (5oz) caster sugar

For the brandy syllabub:
½ lemon
150ml (5fl oz) white wine
1 tbsp brandy
40g (1½oz) caster sugar
300ml (½ pint) double cream

To make the granita, warm 450ml (15fl oz) of the water and blend the coffee granules into it. Add the sugar, bring to the boil and simmer over a low heat for 5 minutes. Leave to cool, adding the remaining water. Pour into a shallow plastic container or metal tray and place in the freezer for about 2 hours. When the mixture has frozen round the edges, take it out of the freezer and scrape it with a fork so that the ice crystals form. Return to the freezer and repeat two or three times, so that the mixture has a rough, granular texture.

To make the syllabub, pare the zest thinly from the lemon and squeeze out the juice. Put the lemon zest, juice, white wine and brandy in a large bowl, cover and leave to infuse for at least 3 hours. Strain into a large bowl, then add the sugar, cover and leave until dissolved. Whip the double cream and, once it becomes lightly aerated, gradually add the liquid so that it holds its shape. Do not over whip or it may curdle. Then chill.

To serve, spoon the granita into chilled goblets and top with the syllabub.

Picnic by the River Am

Chicken and lime mayonnaise sandwiches

Egg, tuna and parsley pitta pockets

Coconut flapjacks

Homemade lemon cordial

Iced Earl Grey tea

May 198

Down by the listlessly flowing, silvery Am, mayflies hovering and swallows swooping, Kate, Debbie and I spread our blanket under drooping, pale willows.

The girls, carefree then and innocent, running barefoot through the long cool grass, spotted minnows and darting sticklebacks. They threaded buttercups and daisies into chains, no Alice then to spoil their games. And when our hunger and our wicker-hamper fare was gone we slowly followed the path by Lyttleton Brook back home.

SUMMER

The stagnant heat of summer fills the village vale with lingering scents of freshly-mown hay. Heady honeysuckle and blowzy full-blown roses tangle and tumble listlessly down old cottage walls. Out in the ochre fields, combines drone and whine, while brown-armed workers long to soothe their dusty throats with draughts of quenching cordials. Lazy picnickers lie on Lakey Hill. Then suddenly, from a lowering cloud, plop upon plop of heavy drops of rain begin to fall, patterning the sandy paths and hinting at an evening's welcome cool.

Robert's Comforting Spinach and Coriander Roulade

Robert Snell must have the patience of a saint to be constantly swept along by Lynda's forceful views. At least he can sneak away occasionally to spend some time with his grandson, Oscar.

SERVES 6

900g (2lb) fresh spinach
4 eggs, separated
15g (½oz) butter, melted
175g (6oz) soft cheese with garlic and herbs
2 tbsp crème fraîche
2 tbsp chopped coriander
salt and pepper

Preheat the oven to 200°C/400°F/Gas 6. Grease a 33 x 23cm (13 x 9in) Swiss roll tin and line the base with non-stick baking parchment. Wash the spinach and discard the stalks. Put in a large saucepan with just the water clinging to its leaves and cook over a low heat for 5 minutes, until wilted and tender. Drain thoroughly and then chop very finely or purée in a food processor. Add the egg yolks, melted butter, season and stir until smooth.

Whisk the egg whites until stiff but not dry, and fold them into the spinach mixture. Immediately spread in the prepared tin and bake for 10–15 minutes, until springy to the touch. Turn out on to a sheet of non-stick parchment and carefully peel off the lining paper, then leave to cool.

Prepare the filling by placing the soft cheese in a bowl and stirring in the crème fraîche and coriander until you have a smooth, creamy mixture that is easy to spread. Add the salt and pepper if necessary and spread the filling on the roulade. Carefully roll up from the short end, using the non-stick parchment underneath to help. Serve cut into slices, garnished with mixed salad leaves.

The perfect accompaniment to a mixed leaf salad supper by our limpid pool, with a glass or two of something chilled and white to settle the dust of harvesting. A supremely relaxing end to a farmer's tiring day.

Olive, Rosemary and Mozzarella Focaccia

'Brush the loaves with olive oil, sprinkle on the sea salt and rosemary and bake for about 30 minutes'

MAKES 2 SMALL LOAVES

350g (12oz) strong plain flour

1 tsp salt

1 sachet easyblend yeast

175g (6oz) mozzarella cheese, cubed

175g (6oz) green olives, stoned and chopped

2 tbsp olive oil, plus extra for brushing

about 175ml (6fl oz) warm water

1 tbsp sea salt

1 tbsp chopped fresh rosemary leaves

MIX THE FLOUR, salt and yeast together in a bowl, stir in the mozzarella and olives and make a well in the centre. Add the olive oil and enough water to make a soft but manageable dough. Turn out on to a floured board and knead lightly for 5–8 minutes, until smooth and elastic, flouring your hands to prevent the dough sticking. Shape into two round flat loaves about 1cm (½ in) thick. Place the loaves on an oiled baking sheet, and leave, covered, in a warm place for about 1½–2 hours, until doubled in size.

Preheat the oven to 200°C/ 400°F/Gas 6. Brush the loaves with olive oil, sprinkle on the sea salt and rosemary and bake for about 30 minutes, until they are risen and sound hollow when tapped on the base.

Kathy's Crunchy Vegetable Crisps

Not happy with Ruairi constantly pushing his little fist into bags of salt and vinegar, barbecued beef or cream cheese and chive flavoured crisps, I've asked Kathy for the really healthy recipe she devised some years ago for her customers at The Bull. Parsnips, sweet potatoes, beetroot and celeriac are ideal vegetables to use.

Peel the vegetables and slice them very thinly, either with a food processor slicing disc or a mandolin. Pat them dry if necessary. Half fill a deep pan with corn or vegetable oil and heat to sizzling point. Drop in a few vegetable slices at a time and fry for just a few seconds, until crisp and golden. Remove and drain on kitchen paper. Grind a little sea salt on them and, when cold, store in an airtight container.

Poor Person's Caviar

Evocatively Mediterranean. Imagine the sound of goats' bells tinkling down the mountainside, the smell of wild thyme, a dishful of black olives.

SERVES 4–6

3 large aubergines
90ml (3fl oz) extra virgin olive oil
juice of 1 large lemon
3 garlic cloves, peeled and crushed
3 tbsp plain yoghurt
salt and pepper

Grill the aubergines until the skins are blackened all over, turning them as necessary. Leave until cool enough to handle and then peel them. Very finely chop the flesh, then beat in the oil, lemon juice, garlic, yoghurt and some seasoning to taste. Turn the mixture into a bowl and chill. Serve with Kathy's Crunchy Vegetable Crisps.

Jean-Paul's Provençal Pie

I think most of Ambridge learned a great deal from Jean-Paul's Gallic kitchen skills and his professional Provençal cuisine.

SERVES 8

2 aubergines, diced

olive oil

4 courgettes, diced

1 large red pepper, deseeded and sliced

2 onions, peeled and sliced

5 tomatoes, skinned and chopped

2 garlic cloves, peeled and crushed

1 tbsp tomato paste

a few sprigs of thyme

small handful of basil leaves

2 bay leaves

10 sheets of filo pastry

55g (2oz) butter, melted

salt and pepper

Put the diced aubergines in a colander, sprinkle them liberally with salt and leave for an hour. Rinse away the bitter juices and dry the aubergines on kitchen paper. Heat a good layer of olive oil in a large frying pan and fry the aubergines until golden, then remove from the pan. Add a little more oil, if necessary, and fry the courgettes until golden, then remove them from the pan, too. Fry the red pepper and onions until the onions are translucent and soft, adding the tomatoes shortly before the end of cooking. Transfer all the vegetables to a large saucepan, stir in the garlic, tomato paste, a few tablespoons of water and the herbs. Season to taste, then cover and simmer for 20–30 minutes, stirring from time to time, until the vegetables are tender but not mushy. Leave to cool.

Preheat the oven to 190°C/375°F/Gas 5. Use half the filo sheets to line a 23cm (9in) springform cake tin or loose-based tart tin, brushing melted butter between each layer. Spoon the cooled vegetables into the pastry case, then place the remaining pastry sheets loosely on top, brushing each one with butter again. Fold the edges of the lower sheets up over the top sheets and brush with more melted butter.

Bake for 25–30 minutes, until the pastry is golden and crisp. Serve warm.

Pat's Pork and Apricot Picnic Pies

There's plenty of Tom's pork at Bridge Farm for Pat to create a delicious filling for these little pack-a-snack meat pies. Perfect for Market Day elevenses with a flask of coffee. Or ideal served warm for supper, especially with creamed celeriac.

MAKES 8 INDIVIDUAL PIES

1 tbsp sunflower oil

1 onion, peeled and finely chopped

450g (1lb) pork fillet, trimmed and diced

115g (4oz) ready-to-eat dried apricots, chopped

2 plump garlic cloves, peeled and finely chopped

a few sage leaves, chopped, or 1 tsp dried sage

1 leek, trimmed and finely chopped

1 egg, beaten, to glaze

salt and pepper

For the hot water crust pastry:

450g (1lb) plain flour

1 tsp salt

200g (7oz) lard

200ml (7fl oz) water

To make the pastry, sift the flour and salt together into a bowl and make a well in the centre. In a saucepan, melt the lard in the water, bring to the boil, then pour into the well. Beat the mixture to a soft dough and knead for a minute. Cover and leave for 30 minutes for the dough to become more elastic.

Meanwhile, make the filling. Heat the oil in a large frying pan and fry the onion until soft but not brown. Add the meat and fry until brown, then add the apricots, garlic and sage, cover and cook gently for 10 minutes. Finally stir in the leeks and some salt and pepper and cook for a further 5 minutes. Turn out on to a plate to cool.

Preheat the oven to 180°C/350°F/Gas 4. Divide the pastry into 8 pieces and roll out two-thirds of each to line eight 10cm (4in) flan tins. Roll out each remaining third to form the pastry lids. Spoon the cooled mixture into each tin. Moisten the edges of the pastry lids and use to cover the pies, pressing the edges together to seal. Brush with the beaten egg and pierce a hole in the centre of each pie. Bake for 30–40 minutes, until a golden brown.

Sage – Sauge

Evergreen herb

Grows in a sunny spot

Use sparingly with port, goose and duck, sausages and broad beans

JUNE

CREAMY COFFEE SPONGE

8oz butter or margarine
4oz sugar
3 eggs, beaten
4 tbsp coffee essence
2 tbsp golden syrup
1lb self-raising flour

For the buttercream:
6oz icing sugar
6oz butter
2 tsp coffee essence

Cream the butter and sugar until pale and fluffy, then gradually add the eggs. Beat well until smooth. Add the coffee essence and syrup, and gently fold in the flour. Divide into three greased sandwich tins and bake at 350ºF for 20 minutes, until springy to the touch. Remove from the tins and cool on a wire rack.

When the sponges are cool, make the buttercream. Sift the icing sugar into a bowl and beat in the butter until the mixture is light and creamy. Mix in the coffee essence, then spread on to the sponges and put together.

1 SUN	**2** MON
3 TUE	**4** WED
5 THU	**6** FRI
12 THU	**13** FRI

19 THU	**20** FRI	**21** SAT	**22** SUN	**23** MON
25 WED	**26** THU	**27** FRI	**28** SAT	**29** SUN

HAYMAKERS' EGG AND PARSLEY PIE

2oz butter, in cubes
4oz plain flour
pinch of salt
2–3 tbsp cold
    water
4–6 eggs

Rub the fat, flour and salt together until the mixture resembles breadcrumbs. Using a knife, gradually add enough water to make a smooth paste. Wrap in parchment and put in the cold store for 15 minutes.

Roll out and line a shallow baking tin with the pastry. Prick the pastry base with a fork, then break in the whole eggs. Sprinkle in a generous handful of chopped fresh parsley and season with salt and pepper. Place a pastry lid on the top and bake in a moderate oven until crisp. Excellent eaten cold.

7 AT	**8** SUN	**9** MON	**10** TUE	**11** WED
4 AT	**15** SUN	**16** MON	**17** TUE	**18** WED

24
 UE

 IDSUMMER'S AY

30
 ON

SPICED RHUBARB PUDDING

6oz cooked rhubarb
2oz butter or
    margarine
2oz sugar
1 egg, beaten
4oz flour
1 tsp ground ginger
½ tsp baking powder
pinch of salt

Grease a pie dish and pour in the cooked rhubarb. Beat the butter and sugar together until pale and fluffy. Add the egg, flour, ginger, baking powder and salt. Stir until well blended.

Spread the mixture over the stewed rhubarb and cook at 400ºF for 20–25 minutes. Serve with custard.

Elsie Catcher's Early Summer Cordial

Elsie Catcher, Ambridge's village school headmistress, came to look after Lilian and me when Mum was away in hospital. Dumpy and rather dull, I thought she was, but Dad was terribly impressed by her organ playing. Mum still sniffs in a snooty way if we ever mention her name.

Pick the creamy white corymbs of elderflower early in the day. Shake any insects off the blossom, snip the flowers from their stalks and put them in a large saucepan. Cover them with cold spring water and simmer for 20 minutes, then strain the liquid carefully through a muslin cloth. Measure it, then return it to the pan with 450g (1lb) of white sugar for every 750ml (1¼ pints) liquid. Heat slowly to dissolve the sugar, then boil rapidly for 4–5 minutes. After it has cooled, bottle and cork. Keep for 2 weeks before using. Dilute to serve.

Mabel Larkin's Dandelion Wine

Those were the days when Mabel and Ned Larkin lived in Woodbine Cottage. Holly-blue butterflies fluttered in the sunlight, lady's-smocks clothed the grassy banks and meadows were dusted with the bright yellow of dandelions.

MAKES ABOUT 3½ LITRES (8 PINTS)

3.5 litres (6 pints) water
225g (8oz) fresh dandelion flowers
25g (1oz) ginger root
1.3kg (3lb) granulated sugar
juice of 1 lemon and 1 orange
15g (½oz) yeast

Bring the water to the boil, then add the dandelion flowers and the ginger. Put to one side and, when cool, cover with a saucepan lid or foil. Leave to stand for 4 days, stirring twice a day.

Strain the liquid through a muslin cloth, being sure to squeeze the flowers in the cloth. Stir the sugar, citrus fruit juice and yeast into the strained liquid. Cover well, and place in a warm room to ferment for around 2 weeks. When the initial fermentation is over (you will know the fermentation process is complete when there are no longer any bubbles on the surface), stir the wine well and allow it to settle for 3 days.

Strain through the muslin one last time, and pour it into bottles. Cork tightly and leave to mature for 6 months.

Lynda's Sage Liqueur

Lynda was ecstatic when she discovered this sophisticated recipe in an old book she had bought from a brocante on a visit to France. 'I've so much sage and it's smothered in flowers'. She picks a good handful of sage leaves and blue flowers.

450ml eau-de-vie (alcool de 50%)
225g sucre granulé
300ml l'eau

Bi

450ml (15fl oz) of eau-de-vie, 50% strength
225g (8oz) granulated sugar
300ml (½ pint) water

Shake the leaves and flowers well to rid them of insects. Place in a wide-necked jar. Add the eau-de-vie, cover and leave for a week. Dissolve the sugar in the water and add to the eau-de-vie. Seal and store in a cool, dark place. 'A perfect pick-me-up when things are beginning to get me down', she promises as she takes sips from a very small glass.

Mushroom and Coriander Picnic Pâté

Before my first child Adam was born, on early misty mornings I would walk and wonder where life was leading me. In the dew-logged grass I found a patch of perfect, pink-gilled baby mushrooms – their delicate shape perfection. It gave me such a comfort seeing the mystery of nature's new lives.

SERVES 6

55g (2oz) butter
2 tbsp olive oil
1 small onion, peeled and finely
    chopped
1 tsp crushed coriander seeds
450g (1lb) button mushrooms
55g (2oz) fresh white breadcrumbs
225g (8oz) cream cheese
2 tsp lemon juice
salt and pepper
coriander leaves, to garnish

Melt the butter and oil in a pan, add the onion and cook gently until softened. Add the crushed coriander seeds and fry for half a minute. Add the mushrooms and toss them together briefly. They must not be cooked through. Remove from the heat and stir in the breadcrumbs so they soak up any excess liquid. Transfer the mixture to a food processor, adding the cream cheese and lemon juice, and blend until smooth. Season to taste. Turn the pâté into individual ramekin dishes, or one large dish or loaf tin lined with cling film, and chill. Serve with hunks of crusty bread.

Brian's Proudly Potted Trout

With the sensitive encouragement of his step-daughter Debbie, Brian developed the leisure potential of Home Farm with an environmentally friendly trout-fishing lake.

SERVES 8–10

400g (14oz) cooked trout fillets
225g (8oz) butter, softened
2 tbsp lemon juice
½ tsp ground mace
½ tsp freshly grated nutmeg
55g (2oz) clarified butter
salt and pepper

Remove any skin and bones from the trout and flake the flesh into small pieces. Beat in the butter, adding the lemon juice, spices and seasoning, or blend it all together in a food processor. Spoon into a serving dish and level the surface. Melt the clarified butter and pour it over the pâté. Cover with foil and chill before serving.

Sweet and Easy Dried Tomatoes

Halve the tomatoes, sprinkle with salt and place on a baking tray in the oven on the lowest possible heat. Leave all night, then pack them in jars and cover with olive oil. Keep in a cool place.

 HOME FARM, AMBRIDGE, BORSETSHIRE

Broad Bean and Garlic Dip

SERVES 8

450g (1lb) broad beans (preferably young ones), shelled
2 garlic cloves, peeled and crushed
½ tsp ground cumin
2 tbsp lemon juice
4 tbsp olive oil
salt and pepper to taste
2 tbsp chopped parsley

Cook the broad beans in boiling salted water until tender (about 10 minutes) and then drain. Pop the skins off, and tip the beans into a blender with the garlic, cumin and lemon juice. Whizz, adding the olive oil in a gentle stream. Season to taste. Serve in a bowl, sprinkled with parsley and my Olive, Rosemary and Mozzarella Focaccia (see p. 130) for dipping.

Broad Bean
Sew: Feb–May Harvest: Jun–Aug

Salade Provençal

Having spent some of his youth in France, Brian suddenly becomes annoyingly knowledgeable. 'Not tuna and anchovy, Jenny. One or the other, not both!' Well, next time he can jolly well make the salad himself!

SERVES 6–8

4 tbsp olive oil
1 tbsp lemon juice
1 garlic clove, peeled and crushed
pinch of black pepper
2 handfuls of green lettuce leaves
4 or 5 waxy new potatoes, cooked and sliced
12 fine green beans, cooked and halved
tin of tuna steak, drained and forked
55g (2oz) anchovy fillets, halved
4 large tomatoes, cut into wedges
10 black olives, stoned
1 tbsp capers
½ cucumber, peeled, deseeded and cut into small wedges
2 hard-boiled eggs, sliced
small handful of basil leaves, shredded

Combine the olive oil, lemon juice, garlic and pepper, whisking well in a bowl or shaking in a screw-top jar. Cover the base of a large bowl with the lettuce leaves. Scatter the potatoes, beans, tuna, anchovy, tomatoes, olives, capers and cucumber over the leaves. Drizzle with the dressing and decorate with the egg and a scattering of basil leaves.

JOE'S COUNTRY JOTTINGS

Set mowers a mowing
on Midsummer's Day
The longer now standing
the worse be the hay

Tarte aux Cerises

Ian says he's looking forward to Home Farm's cherry crop being ready in a few years, so I thought I would pass on this excellent recipe to him.

SERVES 10–12

2 tbsp redcurrant jelly
200g (7oz) crème fraîche
150g (5oz) mascarpone cheese
2 tbsp Armagnac
700g (1½lb) cherries, stoned
1 tbsp icing sugar

For the pastry:
250g (9oz) plain flour
small pinch of salt
140g (5oz) unsalted butter
100g (3½oz) icing sugar, plus extra
    for dusting
1 egg
2 tsp Armagnac

To make the pastry, sift the flour and salt into a large bowl and add the butter. Work together with your fingertips until it resembles fine breadcrumbs. Add the icing sugar and mix together. Beat the egg and Armagnac together, and pour into the flour. Mix with a knife to form a ball. (Alternatively, it is much quicker to make the pastry in a food processor, simply by pulsing the flour and butter, then adding all of the other ingredients until it is all combined.) Wrap the pastry ball in cling film and refrigerate for half an hour.

Preheat the oven to 180°C/350°F/Gas 4. Roll out to 5mm thickness and use to line a 25cm (10in) flan ring. Line the pastry case with greaseproof paper and baking beans, and bake blind for 10 minutes. Remove the paper and beans, and continue cooking for another 5–10 minutes until golden and cooked through.

Meanwhile, make the filling. Melt the redcurrant jelly in a saucepan, stirring frequently, and brush it over the pastry base. Whip together the crème fraîche and mascarpone, adding the Armagnac at the end. Spoon the mixture into the pastry case and pile on the cherries. Sprinkle the tart with icing sugar to decorate.

GREY GABLES
COUNTRY HOUSE HOTEL

Afternoon Tea Menu

SELECTION OF DAINTY SANDWICHES
MUSTARD AND CRESS
SHRIMP
SMOOTH PÂTÉ

•

JEAN PAUL'S FRENCH BERRY TARTLETS

•

DARK CHOCOLATE ECLAIRS

•

EARL GREY OR ASSAM TEA

June 199

There's a table daintily set, with prettily-patterned china and crisp cotton napkins, over there in the window with a wide and wonderful view of springtime greens and chestnut spires beyond. But what else would you expect for wealthy West Midlander Jack Woolley, and his new wife Peggy, proud owner of this Grey Gables Country House Hotel? Smoothly swinging doors reveal, in a pristine kitchen, a short but tall-hatted chef artistically adding a professional touch of 'je ne sais quoi' to his 'petites tartlettes et eclairs chocolat'.

Phoebe's Fluffy Herb Omelette

I can't tell you how happy I was to see Kate and her darling daughter Phoebe together again, and rustling up a quick and easy supper before taking her back to the Tucker's.

SERVES 1

2 eggs
1 heaped dessert spoon of fresh (or 1 tsp of dried) mixed herbs, chopped or snipped
a walnut-sized lump of butter
salt and pepper

Break the eggs carefully into a bowl and beat them with a fork or a whisk. Add the herbs and season well. Heat the butter in a small frying pan, or omelette pan, until it melts. When it starts to sizzle, pour in the egg mixture. Leave it to settle, then move the mixture around gently, pushing it in from the edges of the pan with a spatula. When the underside has begun to turn a golden colour (you can peel back an edge to peek), fold it in half. Carefully turn it out on to a warm plate.

Before folding in half, you could try adding different fillings, such as grated cheese, chopped ham or ginger and beansprouts.

JOHN TREGORRAN'S
HISTORICAL HINTS
Cottagers placed their beehives in a sunny spot by lovage, mignonette, thyme and lavender for the most scented honey

Sizzly Courgette Sticks

450g (1lb) small courgettes
3 tbsp olive oil
salt and pepper
grated Cheddar, or Borsetshire, cheese, to serve

Top and tail the courgettes, then slice them lengthways into sticks. Heat the oil in a frying pan. Add the courgettes and turn them when they are golden and beginning to soften – about 2–3 minutes on each side. Divide the courgettes into 3 or 4 portions, season, and serve with some grated cheese on top.

Sautéed Spinach and Cashew Nuts

Using crinkly green spinach leaves from Ian's prolific vegetable patch and a packet of scrunchy cashew nuts from the village shop, Kate astonished us all with this delicious vegetarian side dish. Eventually, stories about Popeye encouraged little Ruairi to gobble up his, too.

SERVES 6

450g (1lb) fresh spinach
4 tbsp olive oil
3 garlic cloves, peeled and chopped
55g (2oz) cashews
2 tbsp raisins
grated nutmeg
salt and pepper
Parmesan shavings

Wash the spinach thoroughly in cold water. Put the olive oil into a wok and warm gently. Add the garlic, stir well, then add the nuts and the spinach leaves. Stir fry until the spinach wilts, but don't let it go mushy. Add the raisins and a good grating of nutmeg and season well to taste. Stir thoroughly and serve immediately with the Parmesan shavings.

JULY

SUMMER GREEN GOOSEBERRY PIE

5oz butter or margarine
4 tbsp milk
12oz flour
1lb small green gooseberries
½lb sugar

Melt the butter in the milk but do not boil. Pour while hot into the flour and knead well. Line a loose-bottomed cake tin with two-thirds of the pastry, working the dough carefully up the sides. Add the gooseberries and sugar. Roll the remaining pastry as a lid for the pie, with a hole to allow the steam to escape (an up-turned egg cup will do the trick). Bake at 350ºF for about an hour.

1 TUE	**2** WED
3 THU	**4** FRI
5 SAT	**6** SUN

12 SAT	**13** SUN	**14** MON	**15** TUE ST SWITHIN'S DAY	**16** WED
19 SAT	**20** SUN	**21** MON	**22** TUE	**23** WED
26 SAT	**27** SUN	**28** MON	**29** TUE	**30** WED

ANGLER'S SALMON SURPRISE

2oz rice
1 small tin salmon, or tail of fresh
  salmon
1 egg, beaten
a few breadcrumbs
1oz dripping
parsley

Boil the rice in salted water for 20 minutes. Drain and mix with the flaked salmon. Form into cutlets, brush over with egg, roll thickly into breadcrumbs and fry in boiling fat to a golden brown. Serve with fried parsley.

7 MON	**8** TUE *Lilian's birthday*	**9** WED	**10** THU	**11** FRI *Gran's Birthday*
17 THU	**18** FRI			
24 THU	**25** FRI			
31 THU				

STUFFED SUMMER CABBAGE

1 summer cabbage
1lb minced pork (lean)
2oz butter
¼lb cooked rice
1 egg
1 onion, peeled and minced
pinch dried herbs

Separate the leaves of the cabbage, keeping the larger leaves whole for stuffing. Mince the remainder of the the cabbage and boil in salted water for 8 minutes, allowing to steam for 8 minutes longer with the lid on the pan. Strain the cabbage thoroughly.

Mix the minced meat with the rice, egg and onion. Mix and season well. Stew on the hob for 1½ hours.

Grease a dish and put a layer of minced cabbage on the bottom, then fill each large leaf with stuffing and a sprinkling of herbs. Cover with the remainder of the cabbage and dot with butter. Lay the leaves on the minced cabbage and bake in a medium oven until the leaves are tender.

Sweet, sharp, scrunchy and sugary, I was convinced that Lilian bought this dessert frozen from Underwoods' fine food department. But she swore she found the recipe in a stylish magazine while having her highlights done – and passed me the cutting to prove it.

LEMON ROULADE

SERVES 6

4 egg whites
175g (6oz) caster sugar
300ml (½ pint) double cream
3 tbsp lemon curd

For the chocolate sauce:
115g (4oz) plain chocolate
55g (2oz) icing sugar, sifted
300ml (½ pint) double cream
2 tbsp brandy

PREHEAT THE OVEN to 150°C/ 350°F/Gas 2). Grease a 25 x 30cm (10 x 12in) Swiss roll tin and line it with non-stick baking parchment. Whisk the egg whites until they form soft peaks, then gradually whisk in the sugar until smooth, thick and glossy. Spread the mixture lightly and evenly in the tin and bake for 25–30 minutes, until the meringue is firm to the touch. Turn out on to a sheet of parchment paper, carefully peel off the lining paper and leave to cool.

Whip the double cream to soft peaks and fold in the lemon curd. Spread on to the meringue and roll up carefully.

To make the sauce, break up the chocolate and melt it in a bowl set over a pan of hot water, making sure the water is not touching the base of the bowl. Stir in the icing sugar, cream and brandy and leave to cool. Serve the roulade in slices, accompanied by the chocolate sauce.

Lower Loxley's Lime and Lemon Cheese

Apparently this was one of dear Nigel's nursery favourites, spread thickly on healthy brown bread for a tea-time treat, or sandwiched in slices of Nanny's fatless sponge.

MAKES ABOUT 450G (1LB)

grated zest and juice of 3 lemons
grated zest and juice of 2 limes
115g (4oz) unsalted butter, cut into cubes
350g (12oz) caster sugar
4 eggs, lightly beaten

Put the lemon and lime zest and juice into a bowl with the butter and sugar, then strain in the eggs. Set the bowl over a pan of gently simmering water, making sure the water is not touching the base of the bowl, and stir with a wooden spoon until the sugar has dissolved and the butter has melted. Continue to cook, stirring, for 15–20 minutes, until the mixture thickens enough to coat the back of the spoon. Do not overcook or the eggs may curdle. Pour into sterilised jars and seal while hot. When completely cool, store in the refrigerator. Use within 4–6 weeks.

SIMPLE RED BERRIED TART

SERVES 8

3 TBSP REDCURRANT JELLY
300ML (½ PINT) CRÈME FRAÎCHE
225G (8OZ) FRESH RASPBERRIES
225G (8OZ) FRESH STRAWBERRIES

FOR THE PASTRY:
150G (5OZ) UNSALTED BUTTER
75G (3OZ) CASTER SUGAR
1½ TSP ALMOND ESSENCE
1 TBSP WATER
225G (8OZ) PLAIN FLOUR

To make the pastry, melt the butter in a heavy-based saucepan and add the sugar, letting it dissolve but not boil. Remove from the heat, add the almond essence and water, and gradually work in the flour to make a dough. Press the dough with your fingers over the base and halfway up the sides of a buttered 25cm (10in) loose-bottomed flan tin. Prick the base and chill for 15 minutes. Preheat the oven to 160°C/325°F/Gas 3.

Bake the pastry for about 20 minutes, watching it carefully towards the end as it burns easily. When it is pale golden, remove from the oven and leave to cool.

Melt the redcurrant jelly in a small pan over a low heat and brush a thin layer of it over the pastry. Leave for a few minutes, then spread with the crème fraîche. Arrange the berries over the cream and brush with the remaining redcurrant jelly to glaze. Serve in a pool of Red Berry Coulis (see right).

'Arrange the berries over the cream and brush with redcurrant jelly to glaze...'

RED BERRY COULIS

Whizz 225g (8oz) mixed strawberries and raspberries in a blender. Strain through a sieve, then stir in ½ teaspoon of lemon juice and 75g (3oz) caster sugar, or to taste.

Brian has always had a strange weakness for flaming redheads and horsey Mandy Beesborough proved to be no exception.

Lettie's Lavender Shortbread

Mauve and grey clumps of sweet-smelling lavender bloomed in the gardens of Glebe Cottage, reminding Gran of Lettie Lawson-Hope. Lettie, to whom she was in service, bequeathed this little thatched cottage to my grandmother and she and Grandad lived happily there in retirement.

MAKES 12 BISCUITS

1 tbsp lavender flowers
1 tbsp granulated sugar
175g (6oz) plain flour
115g (4oz) unsalted butter
55g (2oz) caster sugar

Preheat the oven to 160°C/325°F/Gas 3. Grind the lavender flowers with the granulated sugar in a spice mill or a coffee grinder, then stir this dark, aromatic mixture into the flour. Cream the butter and caster sugar together until light and fluffy. Add the lavender flour and stir until the mixture binds together. Press into a greased 18cm (7in) round tin and bake for about 40 minutes, until pale golden. Leave the shortbread to cool in the tin, then cut into pieces to serve.

The Orangery's Frilled Florentines

Naughtily more-ish and admittedly delicious with a cup of frothy coffee. Power-walking is on the agenda afterwards to work off those excess calories!

MAKES 12

75g (3oz) **unsalted butter**
55g (2oz) **caster sugar**
25g (1oz) **glacé cherries, chopped**
25g (1oz) **crystallised pineapple, chopped**
40g (1½oz) **macadamia nuts, chopped**
2 tbsp **double cream**
25g (1oz) **candied peel, chopped**
25g (1oz) **raisins**
15g (½oz) **plain flour**
115g (4oz) **good-quality plain chocolate**

Preheat the oven to 180°C/350°F/Gas 4. Grease a baking sheet. Melt the butter in a saucepan, add the sugar and heat gently until dissolved, then bring to the boil. Remove from the heat and stir in all the remaining ingredients except the chocolate. Place heaped teaspoonfuls of the mixture on the baking sheet, spaced well apart. Bake for 8–10 minutes, until the biscuits have spread and are golden brown. Leave to cool for a few minutes, then transfer to a wire rack to cool completely.

Break up the chocolate and melt it in a bowl set over a pan of hot water, making sure the water is not touching the base of the bowl. Stir until smooth. Roll the edges of the biscuits in the chocolate and place them on a sheet of non-stick baking parchment until set.

Little Abbie's Gingerbread Animals

On a dull, damp day Phoebe and Hayley cheered themselves up in the warm kitchen by baking a batch of spicy biscuits. Little Abbie helped by putting in the eyes – and popping them into her mouth when they weren't looking.

350g (12oz) **plain flour**
1 tsp **bicarbonate of soda**
1 tsp **ground ginger**
1 tsp **ground cinnamon**
115g (4oz) **butter or hard margarine**
175g (6oz) **muscovado sugar**
4 tbsp **golden syrup**
1 **egg, beaten**
currants, to decorate

Sift the dry ingredients into a bowl and rub in the butter or margarine until the mixture resembles breadcrumbs. Stir in the sugar. Add the syrup and egg and mix to soft dough. Knead lightly until smooth, then cover and chill for 30 minutes. Preheat the oven to 160°C/325°F/Gas 3.

Roll out the dough to about 3–5mm (¼in) thick and cut out shapes with a non-fluted scone cutter or fancy cutters. Assemble the shapes to resemble animals and decorate with currants. Place on greased baking sheets and bake for 10–15 minutes, until golden. Cool on the baking sheets for 5 minutes and then transfer to a wire rack to cool.

Sipho's Sticky Koeksisters

While on the webcam to South Africa one Sunday evening, little Sipho and Nolly were caught on camera with shiny sugary lips and licking their syrupy fingers. Lucas promised faithfully they would have baths before bedtime and Kate promised Phoebe she would make some of the sticky buns for us before she went home.

MAKES 16

450g (1lb) self-raising flour
½ tsp salt
2 tbsp baking powder
55g (2oz) butter, grated
1 egg, beaten
125ml (4fl oz) water
125ml (4fl oz) milk
1 egg, beaten, to glaze
corn oil, for frying

For the syrup:
500ml (16fl oz/1 pint) water
grated zest and juice
    of 1 lemon
2 cinnamon sticks
1.1kg (2lb) caster sugar

First, make the syrup by combining all of the ingredients in a saucepan. Stir well, then heat gently until all of the sugar has dissolved. Allow to simmer for 10 minutes until it starts to become thicker, then remove from the heat and leave to cool completely.

Sift the dry ingredients into a bowl and rub in the butter using your fingertips. Add the egg and mix, then combine the water and milk in a jug. Add enough of the water and milk mixture to make a soft, scone-like dough. Knead gently on a lightly-floured surface until bubbles start to appear in the dough. Place the dough in a bowl, cover with a damp tea towel and leave to rest for 30 minutes–1 hour.

Roll the dough out to about 1cm (½in) thickness, then cut into oblongs. Divide each oblong into three for plaiting. Brush with the beaten egg to help the strands stick together, then plait the oblongs, pinching the three strands together at the top and bottom so that they don't fall apart.

Heat your oil to boiling point, and test that it's ready by dropping a small amount of the dough into the oil. If it sizzles immediately, the oil is ready. Fry the koeksisters until golden brown, then remove from the oil and blot the excess fat on kitchen paper.

Divide your syrup into two batches, and put one batch in the fridge. Dip the koeksisters into the syrup while they're still warm so that the syrup seals on the outside and leaves the inside dry. If the syrup becomes too warm and thin as you dip more of your koeksisters, change it for the one in the fridge.

Sean's Welsh Tea Bread

Charming Sean, who once ran the Cat & Fiddle, passed his old mum's recipe on to me. Just the thing to pack up in a picnic for a day at the Royal Welsh Show. Don't forget a flask of tea to go with it.

MAKES A 900G (2LB) LOAF

350g (12oz) **mixed dried fruit**
115g (4oz) **soft brown sugar**
150ml (5fl oz) **strong black tea**
225g (8oz) **self-raising flour**
2 tsp **mixed spice**
2 **eggs**

Soak the dried fruit and sugar in the cold tea overnight. The next day, preheat the oven to 180°C/350°F/Gas 4 and grease and line the base of a 900g (2lb) loaf tin. Sift the flour and spice together. Beat the eggs into the fruit and tea mixture, then add the flour and stir to mix all the ingredients thoroughly. Turn into the prepared loaf tin and make a slight dip in the centre. Bake for 1½–1¾ hours or until the loaf is golden brown and a skewer inserted into the centre comes out clean. Cool in the tin for 10 minutes before turning out on a wire rack to cool completely. Store in an airtight tin and keep for at least a day before serving it sliced and spread with butter.

THE ROYAL
WELSH
SHOW

RAMME

The Sterlings' Rich Dessert

Delectably smooth and sophisticated is how I describe this — just like Caroline and Oliver, in fact!

SERVES 6

200g (7oz) good-quality plain chocolate
125ml (4fl oz) double cream
1 tbsp coffee-flavoured liqueur, such as Tia Maria
3 eggs
55g (2oz) caster sugar
icing sugar for dusting

Preheat the oven to 180°C/350°F/Gas 4. Grease and line a 16cm (6½ in) square by 4 cm (1½ in) deep cake tin. Break up the chocolate and melt it in a bowl set over a pan of hot water, making sure the water is not touching the base of the bowl. In a separate bowl, whip the cream to soft peaks, then add the liqueur and gently whisk together.

Whisk the eggs and sugar together until pale and thick. Fold in the melted chocolate, followed by the whipped cream. When all the ingredients are thoroughly mixed, pour into the prepared tin and place in a roasting tin. Fill the roasting tin about three-quarters full with water then place in the oven and bake for 45–60 minutes, or until the cake is firm to a light touch. Leave to cool in the tin, then turn the cake out on a flat plate or a board and dust with sifted icing sugar. Ideally, serve in a pool of Red Berry Coulis (see p. 150) to cut through the richness.

JOE'S COUNTRY JOTTINGS

As harvest approaches
each Lammas Day
Wheat turns brown,
barley silvery-grey

Joe Grundy's Ginger Pop

This ginger pop was drunk by the Grundys at haytime and harvest, and the old recipe has been handed down through generations.

MAKES ABOUT 4.6 LITRES (8 PINTS)

3 lemons, thinly sliced
25g (1oz) fresh ginger root, bruised
450g (1lb) granulated sugar
4.8 litres (8 pints) boiling water
2 tsp brewer's yeast

Put the lemons, bruised ginger root and sugar in a large earthenware crock. Pour on the boiling water and leave until almost cold, then add the yeast. Cover the crock and leave overnight. Strain, then pour into screw-topped bottles, or secure corks with wire. Do not fill the bottles up to the brim. Leave for at least 2 days before using.

The Healthclub's Mint and Grapefruit Sorbet

A refreshing, rejuvenating sorbet. Nothing could be more welcome after a session in the gym or sizzling in the sauna or solarium.

SERVES 4–6

115g (4oz) granulated sugar
300ml (½ pint) water
grated zest and juice of 1 unwaxed lemon
a handful of mint leaves (preferably apple mint) plus a few leaves to garnish
juice of 2 grapefruit
1 egg white

Put the sugar and water into a pan and heat gently, stirring to dissolve the sugar completely. Bring to the boil, add the grated lemon zest and the mint leaves and simmer for 2–3 minutes. Strain into a bowl and leave to cool. Stir the grapefruit and lemon juice into the syrup. Pour into a shallow plastic container or metal tray and freeze. When it has almost frozen through, turn it into a bowl and whisk to break down the ice crystals. In a separate bowl, beat the egg white until stiff and then fold it into the sorbet. Return it to the freezer until firm. Serve in goblets, topped with a mint leaf.

FARMHOUSE FRUIT CAKE

½lb lard and butter, mixed
2lbs self-raising flour
½lb sugar
1 tsp allspice
½lb currants
½lb sultanas
1 tbsp thick marmalade
1 egg, beaten
a little milk, to mix

Rub the lard and butter mixture into the flour and add the sugar, spice and dried dried fruit. Mix together with the marmalade, beaten egg and milk, until the mixture is a stiff consistency. Put into 2 greased and lined loaf tins, and bake at 350ºF for an hour. Test with a skewer to see when cooked (about an hour).

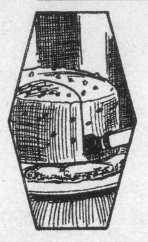

1 FRI	2 SAT
LAMMAS DAY	
5 TUE	
8 FRI	

11 MON	12 TUE		13 WED
	GROUSE SHOOTING BEGINS		

HARVESTER'S CHEESE AND TOMATO PIE

6 slices stale white bread
½ pint milk
4oz grated hard cheese
2oz grated suet
½lb large ripe tomatoes
2oz butter
salt and pepper

Grease a pie dish, soak the bread in the milk. Layer the bread with grated cheese and grated suet. Add a good thick layer of sliced tomatoes, dot with little knobs of butter and season as you go. Top with a layer of bread dotted with butter. Bake in a moderate oven and serve hot.

16 SAT	17 SUN		18 MON
24 SUN	25 MON		26 TUE

3 SUN	4 MON	**RED PLUM TART**

RED PLUM TART

4 eating apples
1lb plums
4oz caster sugar
a little water

For the pastry:
8oz flour
½ tsp cinnamon
4oz butter, or
2oz butter and 2oz lard
3 tsp caster sugar
water to mix

To make the pastry, mix the flour and cinnamon in a bowl and rub in the fat. Add the sugar and, using a knife, mix to a firm paste with the water. Roll out and line a shallow tin with some of the pastry.

For the filling, peel and chop the apples and stone the plums. Mix together with the sugar and place on the pastry. Cover with the remaining pastry and bake for 45 minutes at 350ºF.

6 WED	7 THU
9 SAT	10 SUN
14 THU	15 FRI

19 TUE	20 WED	21 THU	22 FRI	23 SAT
27 WED	28 THU	29 FRI	30 SAT	31 SUN

Wild Cherries in Brandy

This reminded Jean-Paul of the Armagnac region of France. 'Oh, to be in Gascony,' he would sigh.

MAKES 450G (1LB)

450g (1lb) cherries
115g (4oz) light soft brown sugar
about 600ml (1 pint) brandy
a few almonds, blanched and chopped

Wash and dry the cherries and remove the stalks. Prick them all over with a darning needle. Half fill a sterilised wide-necked jar with the cherries and sugar, then nearly fill to the brim with brandy. Add the shredded almonds. Seal and keep for several months before using.

Mediterranean Water Ice

A perfect and refreshing way to cleanse the palate between two rich courses and to remind Brian of the sun sinking behind the mountains in Andalucía.

SERVES 8

115g (4oz) caster sugar
300ml (½ pint) water
finely pared zest and juice of 1 orange
1 ripe honeydew melon
1 tbsp preserved ginger, finely chopped, plus 2 tbsp of the ginger syrup
2 egg whites

Put the sugar and water in a heavy-based pan and heat gently until the sugar has dissolved. Bring to the boil and simmer for 3–4 minutes, until syrupy. Add the orange zest and juice, leave to cool and then strain.

Halve and seed the melon, then purée the flesh in a food processor, adding the ginger syrup and the strained orange syrup. Fold in the chopped ginger, then pour into a shallow plastic container or metal tray and freeze for 2–3 hours, until mushy.

Turn the mixture into a bowl and whisk to break down the ice crystals. Whisk the egg whites until stiff. Fold them into the melon mixture, return it to the container and freeze until firm. Transfer to the fridge an hour before serving.

Bert's Best Tips:
Pick blackcurrants on a warm summer's day

Peggy's Pink Rose Petal Sorbet

Mum still has fond memories of Blossom Hill Cottage – the humble homeliness of it all. The steeply dipping dun-brown thatch, its peeping windows and the garden a comfortable jumble of colourful plants. Stately hollyhocks stood sentinel at the porch, love-in-the-mist spread like a shimmering, vapid haze, while the fragrance of old-fashioned roses scented the evening air.

SERVES 6–8

350g (12oz) granulated sugar
600ml (1 pint) water
3 handfuls of pink and red old-fashioned
    fragrant rose petals
1 tbsp lemon juice
225g (8oz) redcurrants
225g (8oz) whitecurrants

Put the sugar and water in a saucepan and heat gently until the sugar has dissolved. Bring to the boil, reduce the heat and simmer for 5 minutes to make a syrup, then leave to cool. Snip off the white ends from the rose petals, wash the petals and pat dry on paper towels. Put them in a food processor with the lemon juice and 125ml (4fl oz) of the sugar syrup. Blend to a purée.

Purée the currants in the food processor, then sieve to extract the juice. Measure the juice and add to the petal mixture with an equal quantity of the sugar syrup. Pour into a shallow plastic container or metal tray and freeze. Before serving, tip the sorbet into the food processor and blend to form a soft, pink ice. Spoon into tall glasses and serve immediately.

LILIAN'S GLORIOUS RACING TEA

CREAM CHEESE AND CAVIAR BLINIS

ASPARAGUS AND SMOKED
SALMON SANDWICHES

MINI MOCHA PROFITEROLES

CUPCAKES

STRAWBERRY SCONES

PIMM'S

CHAMPAGNE

MINT TEA

July 200.

Imagine you can see a sea of bright and bobbing colourful chip-straw hats. Imagine you can hear the thunder of pounding hooves and the high-pitched guffaws of gregarious gamblers. Imagine you can smell the grassy scent of earthy turf. Posh totties perching perilously on striped aluminium chairs, or lolling lazily on tartan rugs. Hamper picnics packed with Underwoods' delicatessen's delicacies, cooler-chilled and plug-in temperature controlled. All meticulously stowed in the spacial opulence of a greedy gas-guzzling 4X4. That's all in a day in the life of Lilian – one of her specially sociable glorious summer days!

Usha's Fresh Mango and Lime Chutney

Back home from shopping in Borchester's busy market, Usha unpacks a bag of mangoes. Even now, Alan is still in awe when she sets to, chopping the fruit and beating the spices. Soon The Vicarage is filled with spicy, nose tickling smells. What's even better, the chutney is ready to eat for supper, stuffed into homemade paratha.

MAKES ABOUT 450G (1LB)

2 tsp coriander seeds
2 tsp cumin seeds
1 tsp fennel seeds
3 tbsp chopped coriander
3 tbsp chopped mint
2 large ripe mangoes, peeled, stoned and chopped
3 tbsp caster sugar
juice of 3 limes
2 fresh green chillies, chopped
½ tsp salt

Heat the coriander, cumin and fennel seeds in a dry frying pan until they pop. Put the spices into a food processor with all the remaining ingredients and blend to a paste. Spoon into a jar or dish, cover and refrigerate. It should keep for a few days.

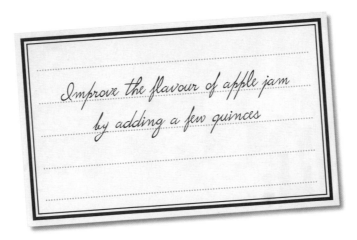

Improve the flavour of apple jam by adding a few quinces

Mrs Antrobus's Colonial Chutney

Thrilled to be able to explain to the hoi polloi that chutney is derived from the Hindustani word chatni, meaning a strong sweet relish, Marjorie happily used to reminisce about Big Game and chukkas of polo, her husband Teddy's postings and their colonial lifestyle. Fascinating ramblings and a fiery chutney. It used to sell terribly well on the WI stall.

MAKES ABOUT 2.5–3 KG (5–6LB)

900g (2lb) cooking apples, cored, 1 peeled and chopped
450g (1lb) onions, peeled and chopped
225g (8oz) ready-to-eat dried apricots, chopped
225g (8oz) dates, chopped
115g (4oz) sultanas
450g (1lb) demerara sugar
1 tbsp salt
1 tbsp mustard powder
½ tsp ground ginger
1 tsp mixed spice
1 tsp curry powder
pinch of cayenne pepper
1.2 litres (2 pints) malt vinegar

Put all the ingredients into a preserving pan and bring to the boil, stirring. Simmer gently for about 2 hours, stirring frequently, until thick, smooth and glossy. Pour into sterilised jars and seal with vinegar-proof tops while hot. Keep for 6 weeks before opening.

Eddie Grundy's Saucy Pickle

I remember years back this savoury relish was concocted specially by Clarrie to spice up the barbecued sausages at Eddie's Country and Western evenings. It's just as tasty on my nephew Tom's sausages as well!

MAKES ABOUT 2.5KG (5LB)

2 large onions, peeled and chopped
2 garlic cloves, peeled and chopped
1 celery stick, chopped
2 large carrots, peeled and diced
450g (1lb) cooking apples, cored, peeled and chopped
450g (1lb) dates, minced
450g (1lb) sultanas
grated zest and juice of 2 oranges
2 tbsp English mustard or Grundy's Fuggle Mustard (see p. 57)
1 tsp ground ginger
600ml (1 pint) malt vinegar
1 tsp salt
1 tsp ground cinnamon
450g (1lb) soft dark brown sugar

Put all the ingredients except the sugar into a preserving pan and bring to the boil, stirring from time to time. Simmer for about 30 minutes, until the vegetables are tender. Add the sugar and stir to dissolve. Simmer for another 20 minutes or until the mixture thickens. Pour into sterilised jars and seal with vinegar-proof tops while hot.

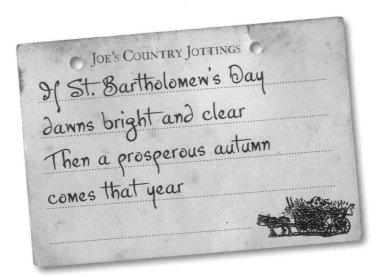

JOE'S COUNTRY JOTTINGS

If St. Bartholomew's Day
dawns bright and clear
Then a prosperous autumn
comes that year

Ralph and Lilian's Rumpot

On those glorious early summer days, when bees are humming and bushes are bowing low with their harvest of soft, sweet berries, it's time to pickle and pot and put away for the winter. At her late husband Ralph's suggestion many moons ago, Lilian would carefully layer soft fruits with sugar and generous splashes of white rum, creating a richly alcoholic dessert for chilly days, which she would top with clotted cream. She also used the fruited rum as a syrupy sweet liqueur — both she and Ralph were frightfully fond of liqueur.

Choose any ripe, soft summer fruits as they come into season – strawberries, raspberries, cherries, apricots, plums – but make sure they are unblemished. Wipe the fruit carefully and remove any stones. Arrange layers of the fruit in a large, sterilised glass jar or earthenware crock, sprinkling each layer with granulated sugar and pouring over a generous amount of rum or brandy. Cover loosely and add more fruit as it comes into season. At the end of the summer, when the crock is full, cover it securely and leave in a cool, dry place to mature.

'Preserve summer fruits to create a richly alcoholic dessert for chilly winter days...'

Redcurrant and Rosemary Jelly

After a long day roaming the Ambridge countryside researching local history with John Tregorran, I cooked a deliciously tender leg of lamb. He was such an old romantic: 'That's rosemary, that's for remembrance,' I remember he said as we wandered through the gardens at Manor Court. Carol was away at the time. Maybe it's just as well that they decided to leave Ambridge and settle in the West Country.

MAKES ABOUT 1.5KG (3LB)

1.1kg (2½lb) redcurrants
600ml (1 pint) water
granulated sugar or preserving sugar
125ml (4fl oz) white wine vinegar
2 tbsp chopped rosemary

Put the redcurrants in a preserving pan with the water and simmer until soft and pulpy. Put the fruit in a jelly bag and leave to drip for at least 2 hours or overnight. Measure the juice, then return it to the pan, adding 450g (1lb) sugar for every 600ml (1 pint) juice. Heat gently, stirring until the sugar dissolves. Bring to the boil, add the vinegar and rosemary and boil rapidly until setting point is reached: to test for this, put a teaspoonful of the jelly on a saucer, place in the fridge for a minute or two and then gently push it with your finger – if it wrinkles, it is ready. Skim off the scum, pour into sterilised jars and seal while hot.

erb Garden

osemary

emary is for remembrance. Both
kespeare and Thomas More
te about the herb referring to its
ociation with remembrance and
refore friendship, and as a plant to
used at funerals as a remembrance

rrying on with the remembrance
eme, rosemary had many
sociations with weddings and love.
veral centuries ago both bride

Fresh Fig and Ginger Conserve

*On one of her town-twinning visits to the market town of Meyruelle,
Lynda couldn't resist returning with a bulging bag of sweet plum figs.
'Robert, the fragrance of France!' And what could be better than capturing
the taste but in a jar of syrupy preserve to savour on a cold, grey, wintry
English day? Choose figs that are not too ripe and still fairly firm.*

MAKES ABOUT 2KG (4LB)

**1.1kg (2½lb) fresh figs
juice of 1 lemon and 1 large orange
1.1kg (2½lb) granulated sugar or preserving sugar
55g (2oz) preserved ginger in syrup, finely chopped
3 tbsp rum**

Prick the figs with a needle, blanch them in boiling water for 1 minute and then drain. Put them in a preserving pan with the lemon and orange juice and simmer for about 15 minutes. Add the sugar and ginger and stir until the sugar has dissolved. Bring to the boil and simmer until the syrup is thick enough to coat the back of a wooden spoon. Add the rum and bring to the boil again. Pour into sterilised jars and seal while hot.

*Bert's Best Tips:
Gather herbs for drying only at a full moon,
at Lammastide (August 1st)*

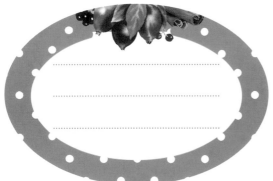

Ingredients Index

Index of Characters and Places

Acknowledgements

My special thanks go to the editor of *The Archers* Vanessa Whitburn for her continued support, and to Kim and Camilla for giving thorough attention to detail.

I am tremendously grateful to my patient and tireless editor Emily Pitcher, who not only deciphered my nearly illegible scrawl but checked my recipes and offered enthusiastic encouragement.

Shaping this book has definitely been a team effort and I owe my thanks to Mary Woodin and Pru Rogers for so enchantingly bringing it to life – not forgetting Tilly and Oscar.

And finally I'm indebted to all the inhabitants of Ambridge, past and present, without whom this book could not have been possible.

Picture Credits